THE CREATIVE COOK

THE CREATIVE COOK

Edited by Eileen Turner

TREASURE PRESS

Contents

First published in 1976 and revised in 1984 by Octopus Books Limited under the title *All Color Cookbook*

This edition published in 1985 by Treasure Press, 59 Grosvenor Street, London W1

© 1976 and 1984 Octopus Books Limited

ISBN 1 85051 095 4

Printed in Hong Kong

Appetizers

Avocado surprise with tuna and cream cheese
Serves 6

3 avocados
1 can (about 7 oz) tuna, drained
1 package (8 oz) cream cheese, room temperature
3 tablespoons lemon juice
shake of pepper
black olives, to garnish

Cut the avocados in half and remove the stones. Scoop out some of the flesh and place it in a small bowl. Add the other ingredients and beat well. Pile the mixture back into the avocado halves and garnish each with an olive.

Avocado surprise with tuna and cream cheese

Avocado cream dip
Serves 4

2 avocados
2 tablespoons lemon juice
3 tablespoons thick mayonnaise
1 very small onion, or 2–3 scallions, finely chopped
2 tablespoons dairy soured cream
2 tablespoons heavy cream
salt and pepper
To garnish
½ cup shelled and deveined shrimp, thawed if frozen

Halve the avocados and remove the stones. Spoon the flesh into a bowl, taking care not to damage the skins. Reserve the skins. Add the lemon juice and mash thoroughly. Blend in all the other ingredients except the shrimp. Pile the mixture in the skins and top with the shelled shrimp.

Melon and pineapple dip
Serves 6

1 canteloup or honeydew melon
2 packages (8 oz each) cream cheese
¾ cup plain yogurt
1 tablespoon concentrated tomato paste
1 can (about 8 oz) pineapple pieces, drained
2 tablespoons finely chopped fresh parsley
salt and pepper

Cut the top off the melon and scoop out the flesh from the piece removed. Remove the seeds and scoop the pulp from the melon; make a few melon balls for decoration.

Blend the cream cheese, yogurt and tomato paste until smooth. Stir in the melon flesh, pineapple pieces and parsley. Mix thoroughly, adding a little of the pineapple syrup if the mixture is too stiff. Season well. Spoon the mixture into the melon case and top with the melon balls; cover with plastic wrap and refrigerate until ready to serve.

Left: Melon and pineapple dip
Centre: Kippered herring and grapefruit dip
Right: Avocado cream dip

Kippered-herring and grapefruit dip
Serves 4

2 lean slices bacon
2 fairly large grapefruit
1½ cups cottage cheese
1 small onion, finely chopped
½ cup heavy cream
2 tablespoons chopped parsley
2 kippered-herring fillets, flaked
salt and pepper

Fry or broil the bacon until crisp. Reserve four pieces for the garnish and finely chop the rest. Halve the grapefruit and scoop out, reserving the skins. Press through a strainer to extract the juice. Mix the juice with the chopped bacon, cottage cheese, onion and cream. Blend thoroughly, then add the parsley and the kippered-herring fillets, reserving four pieces for the garnish. Season the mixture well and pile into the reserved grapefruit shells. Garnish with the reserved bacon and kippered-herring.

Top: Mushroom-rice salad; Centre: Vegetable salad Niçoise; Bottom left: Orange-herring salad; Bottom right: Bean and salami salad

Four simple hors d'oeuvre

Bean and salami salad
Rub the salad bowl with a cut garlic clove. Mix diced salami and cooked lima beans. Toss in oil and vinegar and season well.

To vary, diced frankfurters, ham or garlic sausage may be used instead of salami.

Orange-herring salad
Mix segments of fresh orange with soused or rollmop herrings. Season well. Arrange on a bed of lettuce.

To vary, use portions of smoked trout or smoked mackerel with orange or other fairly sharp fruit. Serve with horseradish sauce.

Vegetable salad niçoise
Mix sliced or quartered tomatoes, tiny cooked whole or sliced new potatoes, diced cooked green beans and black olives. Toss in oil and vinegar and season well.

Mushroom-rice salad
Cook long grain rice in boiling salted water until just tender. Drain and toss in well-seasoned oil and vinegar. Allow to cool, then mix with strips of green pepper, sliced raw button mushrooms and golden raisins.

To vary, add chopped anchovy fillets, pine nuts or blanched almonds; or mix with cooked peas, flaked salmon and diced cucumber.

Raw mushroom salad
Serves 4

3¼ cups button mushrooms
1 garlic clove
½ teaspoon finely grated lemon rind
3 tablespoons olive oil
3 tablespoons lemon juice
pinch of ground nutmeg
salt and pepper
4 tablespoons finely chopped fresh parsley

Wipe the mushrooms clean and cut them into thin slices. Cut the garlic clove in half and rub it around the inside of a wooden or glass salad bowl. Add the lemon rind, oil, lemon juice, nutmeg and salt and pepper. Beat thoroughly to mix. Add the mushrooms and toss gently with a spoon until all the slices are coated with the dressing. Cover and leave to stand at room temperature for 15 minutes.

Serve in individual salad bowls and sprinkle with chopped parsley.

Cauliflower salad
Serves 4 to 6

1 medium-sized cauliflower
8 anchovy fillets, finely chopped
18 ripe black olives, pitted and halved
1 small onion, grated
1 tablespoon capers
⅓ cup olive oil
2 tablespoons lemon juice
1 tablespoon wine vinegar
freshly ground pepper

Break the cauliflower into flowerets and cook in boiling, salted water for 5 minutes. Drain and transfer to a bowl. Cool to lukewarm, then refrigerate for at least 1 hour.

Mix all the remaining ingredients in a bowl. Add the chilled cauliflower and toss thoroughly. Chill for 30 minutes before serving.

Cauliflower salad

Above: Raw mushroom salad
Right: Prosciutto with melon
Below right: Asparagus on artichoke hearts

Prosciutto with melon
Serves 6

1 honeydew or canteloupe melon, chilled
12 slices of prosciutto

Cut the melon into six slices and remove the seeds. Place melon slices on a serving dish and arrange two slices of prosciutto over each one. Alternatively, cut the melon into large cubes (without the skin) and wrap a piece of prosciutto around each cube. Secure with cocktail sticks and serve on a platter.

Asparagus on artichoke hearts
Serves 4

4 globe artichoke hearts
2 lb asparagus
4 hard-boiled eggs
hollandaise sauce

Poach the artichoke hearts, then leave them to cool. Wash and scrape the asparagus and discard the tough part of the stems. Tie the tips in bundles and cook in boiling, unsalted water for 15–20 minutes.

Chop the eggs, mix with some of the asparagus tips and place on the artichoke hearts. Place the remaining asparagus tips on top and pour over the hollandaise sauce.

9

Right: Speedy spiced pâté
Below left: Artichoke vinaigrette
Below right: Frosted tomato cocktail
*Opposite top: Melon balls with
lemon sauce*
Opposite bottom: Stuffed peaches

Artichokes vinaigrette
Serves 4

4 globe artichokes

salt

bottled oil and vinegar dressing

Wash the artichokes in cold salted water. Cut away
any stem and pull off any tough outer leaves. Cut the
leaves in a line with scissors, if wished.

Cook the artichokes in boiling, salted water until
tender. Small, very young artichokes take about 25
minutes, very large ones take about 40 minutes.
When a leaf can be pulled away easily, it is done.
Allow to cool, then remove the center choke.

Serve the dressing separately or spoon it into the
center of each artichoke. To eat artichokes, pull away
each leaf, dip the base in the dressing and eat the
tender part. The base of the artichoke, often called
the heart, is eaten with a knife and fork.

Frosted tomato cocktail
Serves 4 to 6

4 large ripe tomatoes

$\frac{1}{4}$ cup water

salt and pepper

good pinch of sugar

little lemon juice

Worcestershire sauce

sprigs of mint, to garnish

Chop the tomatoes and put them in a pan with the
water, seasoning and sugar. Heat for a few minutes
only to extract the juice from the tomatoes. Rub the
tomatoes through a strainer and add lemon juice,
Worcestershire sauce and any extra seasoning
required (i.e. celery salt, cayenne or chili sauce). Put
into an ice cube tray without the dividers and freeze.

Chop the frozen mixture lightly and spoon into
chilled glasses. Garnish with mint sprigs.

Speedy spiced pâté
Serves 6 to 8

½ lb liverwurst
½ package (4 oz) cream cheese, room temperature
2 tablespoons thick mayonnaise
3 tablespoons heavy cream
1 teaspoon Worcestershire sauce
½ teaspoon curry powder
1 teaspoon brandy or dry vermouth
salt and pepper

Mix all the ingredients until smoothly combined. Place in a pâté mold lined with aluminum foil, or in individual cups, cover with clear plastic wrap or aluminum foil and chill until required.
    Serve with hot buttered toast.

Melon balls with lemon sauce
Serves 4 to 6

1 honeydew melon
2 lemons
little water
3 tablespoons sugar
To garnish
mint sprigs
lemon slices

Halve the melon and remove the seeds. Make melon balls with a melon baller or teaspoon and chill. Keep fragments of melon left at the bottom of the fruit for the sauce.
    Grate enough rind from the lemons to make 2 teaspoons. Squeeze the juice, measure and add enough water to make ¾ cup of liquid. Simmer the rind in the liquid and sugar for about 5 minutes. Add the odd pieces of melon, then strain or purée in a blender. Taste and add more sugar, if desired. Spoon the sauce into 4–6 glasses and top with the melon balls. Garnish with mint and lemon slices.

Stuffed peaches
Serves 4

1 package (8 oz) cream cheese
2 tablespoons golden raisins,
soaked in hot water
2 tablespoons chopped walnuts
2 large ripe peaches, or 4 canned
peach halves
4 crisp lettuce leaves

Mix the cheese, raisins and nuts and form into 12 small balls. If the balls are very soft, chill the mixture for a short time. Arrange each peach half on a lettuce leaf in a small bowl and place three cheese balls on each. Serve chilled.

Above: Pâté de maison; Above right: Chicken liver pâté

Pâté de maison
Serves 6

¾ lb picnic ham joint, boned and rolled
1 tablespoon clear honey
2 teaspoons light soft brown sugar
8 cloves
6 peppercorns
pinch of dried thyme
1 small bay leaf
½ lb pig liver
1 slice brown bread, crust removed
¼ lb pork sausage meat
¼ cup shortening, melted
1 small garlic clove, crushed
grated rind of ½ lemon
1 onion, chopped
pinch of ground allspice
pinch of ground nutmeg
½ teaspoon salt
pinch of pepper
1 egg
1–2 tablespoons dry sherry
1 large lemon or 5 slices of bacon

Put the ham in a saucepan with the honey, sugar, cloves, peppercorns, herbs and sufficient water just to cover. Cover with a lid, bring to a boil and simmer for 35 minutes. Remove the ham from the saucepan and take off the rind. Grind the ham, liver and bread finely, then blend with all the other ingredients except the whole lemon or bacon slices.

Preheat the oven to 325°. Slice the lemon very thinly and use it to line the base and sides of a greased round or oval ovenproof dish. Alternatively, line the dish with the bacon slices. Fill with the pâté, cover with a lid or foil, and place it in a baking pan half filled with hot water. Bake for 2 hours. Allow to cool completely before serving. Serve sliced with hot toast and butter.

Chicken liver pâté
Serves 4

½ lb chicken livers
¼ cup (½ stick) butter, melted
1 tablespoon dry sherry or brandy
1 garlic clove, crushed
pinch of dried thyme
pinch of ground mixed spice
salt
freshly ground black pepper
extra melted butter

Clean the chicken livers well, removing any membrane or tubes. Cook the livers gently in half the butter for 3 minutes; they should still be pink inside. Remove the livers and add the sherry or brandy to the skillet. Remove from the heat.

Mash the livers well with a wooden spoon, add the garlic, the rest of the butter, thyme, mixed spice and a little salt and pepper. Stir in the liquid from the pan and spoon the pâté into a small earthenware bowl. Pour over the extra melted butter. Chill well. Serve with hot toast.

Note: Although chicken liver pâté keeps fairly well, it is best used within 2–3 days of cooking. Always store in the coldest part of the refrigerator until needed.

Shrimp in cream sauce

Serves 4

1½ cups cooked, deveined and shelled shrimp

freshly ground black pepper

pinch of ground nutmeg

3 tablespoons butter

1 tablespoon brandy

¾ cup heavy cream

1 teaspoon finely chopped parsley

To serve

boiled rice

lemon wedges

Season the shrimp with pepper and nutmeg. Melt the butter in a skillet and cook the shrimp over gentle heat for 3 minutes. Warm the brandy in a spoon, set light to it and pour it flaming over the shrimp. When the flames have gone out, reduce the heat to low and cook for 2 minutes. Then increase the heat and add the cream. Cook until the cream thickens, shake the pan and stir the sauce. Stir in the finely chopped parsley.

Serve on hot boiled rice, garnished with lemon wedges as in the photograph (right). Or mix with hot cooked spaghetti or other pasta for a deliciously different pasta sauce.

Above: Shrimp in cream sauce
Below: Shrimp and halibut salad

Shrimp and halibut salad

Serves 4 to 6

¾ lb halibut

salt

1 cup deveined and shelled shrimp, thawed if frozen

¾ cup thick mayonnaise

little lemon juice

1 small green pepper, seeded, sliced and diced

1 small red pepper, seeded, sliced and diced

watercress or lettuce leaves

black olives, to garnish

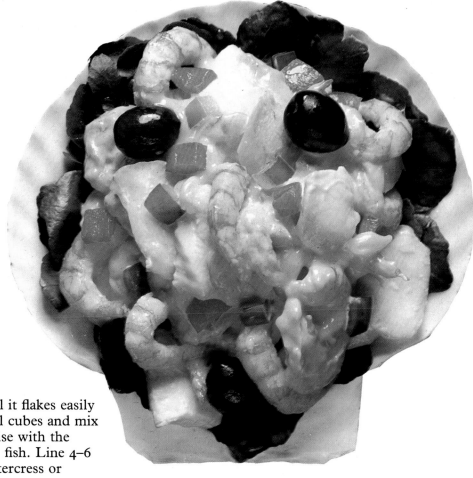

Poach the halibut in salted water until it flakes easily with a fork. Cut the halibut into small cubes and mix it with the shrimp. Mix the mayonnaise with the lemon juice. Add the peppers and the fish. Line 4–6 small dishes or scallop shells with watercress or lettuce leaves. Spoon the fish mixture on top and garnish with black olives.

Soups

Chinese mushroom soup

Serves 4 to 6

3¾ cups home made chicken broth
½ inch slice fresh ginger
2 scallions, thinly sliced
2 cups thinly sliced button mushrooms
1 tablespoon dry sherry
salt and pepper

Left: Chinese mushroom soup
Centre: Chinese shrimp and
egg flower soup
Right: Chinese beef
and vegetable soup

Put the stock in a saucepan with the ginger and scallions. Bring to a boil and simmer for 20 minutes.

Add the mushrooms and simmer for 10 minutes more. Remove the ginger. Add the sherry and season. Serve very hot.

Chinese shrimp and egg flower soup

Serves 4 to 6

2 scallions, finely chopped
3¾ cups home made chicken broth
1½ teaspoons dry sherry
pinch of monosodium glutamate
pinch of sugar
1 teaspoon soy sauce
1½ cups shelled and deveined shrimp, thawed if frozen
1 egg, well beaten
salt

Put the scallions in a large saucepan with the stock. Bring to a boil and simmer, covered, for 10 minutes.

Add the sherry, monosodium glutamate, sugar, soy sauce and shrimp. Reheat gently until the shrimp are heated through. Pour in the egg and stir until it separates into shreds. Add salt to taste. Serve immediately.

Chinese beef and vegetable soup

Serves 4 to 6

¼ lb corned boneless brisket
4 Chinese dried mushrooms
3¾ cups home made beef broth or canned beef consommé
1 tomato, peeled and sliced
2 scallions, sliced
6 water chestnuts, sliced into strips
½ cup canned bamboo shoots, drained and sliced into strips
pinch of monosodium glutamate
salt and pepper

Cut the beef into thin strips across the grain of the meat. Soak the mushrooms in warm water for 20 minutes, rinse, squeeze dry and cut into thin strips, discarding the stems. Put the broth in a large saucepan and bring to a boil. Add the beef and simmer for 4–5 minutes. Add the vegetables and cook for 2 minutes. Add the monosodium glutamate and season. Serve very hot.

Crab bisque
Serves 4 to 6

1 medium-sized cooked crab
2 cups fish broth
1 lemon
freshly ground salt and pepper
bouquet garni
$\frac{1}{4}$ cup ($\frac{1}{2}$ stick) butter
1 onion, chopped
$\frac{1}{2}$ cup sliced mushrooms
$1\frac{1}{4}$ cups light cream
2 egg yolks
2 tablespoons dry sherry, or vermouth

Remove all the meat from the crab, flake it and set aside. Put the shell in a saucepan with the broth, the rind of the lemon, a little lemon juice, seasoning and the bouquet garni. Cover saucepan and simmer gently for 30 minutes. Melt the butter in a large pan and cook the onion and mushrooms. Strain in the crab stock and add the flaked crab meat. Heat gently. Blend the cream with the egg yolks, add to the crab mixture and stir; do not boil. Add the sherry.

Crab bisque

Cauliflower soup

Serves 4 to 6

$\frac{1}{4}$ cup ($\frac{1}{2}$ stick) butter
1 large chopped onion
1 garlic clove, crushed
1 medium-sized cauliflower, in flowerets
$4\frac{1}{2}$ cups chicken broth
salt and pepper
$\frac{1}{4}$ cup light cream
1 tablespoon chopped parsley, to garnish

Melt the butter in a large saucepan. Add the onion and garlic and cook until soft. Add the flowerets of cauliflower and broth. Cover, and simmer for about 1 hour.

Remove the saucepan from heat and beat well with a wire whisk or fork to break up the pieces of cauliflower. Season, stir in cream and reheat gently.

Sprinkle the chopped parsley over the soup just before serving.

Right: Cauliflower soup
Below right: Cream of chicken soup

Cream of chicken soup

Serves 6

2 tablespoons ground rice
$\frac{3}{4}$ cup milk
5 cans ($10\frac{3}{4}$ oz each) condensed chicken broth
lemon juice
ground nutmeg
salt and pepper
2 eggs
2 tablespoons light cream
2 tablespoons finely chopped fresh parsley

Mix the ground rice with the milk until smooth. Heat the broth, add the rice mixture, stir until boiling, then simmer for about 20 minutes.

Season carefully with lemon juice, nutmeg and pepper. Taste before adding salt as the broth may be salty enough. Strain the soup and return it to the saucepan to heat. Beat the eggs, add a little of the hot soup, then add the egg mixture gradually to the soup. Make sure the soup does not boil. Just before serving, stir in the cream and parsley.

Chilled summer soup
Serves 4

3 tablespoons butter
1 medium-sized head lettuce, shredded
½ cucumber, peeled and chopped
1 onion, chopped
grated rind of 2 oranges
3¾ cups chicken broth
3 tablespoons all-purpose flour
salt and pepper
1¼ cups light cream
extra diced cucumber, to garnish
quartered oranges, to serve

Melt the butter in a large saucepan and add the lettuce, cucumber, onion and orange rind. Lower the heat and cook for 10 minutes. Add most of the broth. Simmer gently for 10 minutes. Mix the flour with the remaining broth and stir the mixture into the soup. Cook until the soup has thickened and season well. Purée the soup in a blender, or strain it. Refrigerate the soup until well chilled, then beat in the cream. Serve chilled, topped with diced cucumber and accompanied by orange quarters.

Left: Chilled summer soup
Below left: French onion soup

French onion soup
Serves 4

¼ cup (½ stick) butter
3 large Bermuda onions, thinly sliced
1 tablespoon all-purpose flour
3¾ cups vegetable broth
salt and pepper
To garnish
French bread
grated cheese

Melt the butter in a large, heavy saucepan. Add the onions and cook, stirring constantly, until they are soft and golden. Stir in the flour and cook for 1 minute, then slowly stir in the stock and season. Cover and simmer gently for 20 minutes.

Toast four slices of French bread and sprinkle with grated cheese. Broil until the cheese melts and bubbles. Top each bowl of soup with a slice of cheese-topped toast and serve hot.

Lobster bisque

Serves 6 to 8

$\frac{1}{4}$ cup ($\frac{1}{2}$ stick) butter
1 large carrot, finely chopped
1 large onion, finely chopped
1 small lobster
3 tablespoons brandy
1$\frac{1}{4}$ cups dry white wine
$\frac{1}{2}$ cup rice
7$\frac{1}{2}$ cups fish broth
$\frac{3}{4}$ cup light cream
salt
cayenne
sliced French bread, to serve

Melt half the butter in a large saucepan and add the carrot and onion. Cook gently, stirring, for 2–3 minutes. Split the lobster in half lengthwise, remove the coral and reserve. Place the lobster, cut side down, on the vegetables. Cover the pan and cook for 2 minutes. Heat the brandy, set light to it and pour it over the lobster with the wine. Cover the pan tightly and cook very gently for 15 minutes, lightly shaking the pan occasionally. Cook the rice in 2$\frac{1}{2}$ cups boiling fish broth for about 30 minutes, until very soft.

Shell the lobster, cut up the meat and place it in a bowl with the coral. Add the drained vegetables (reserving the liquid) and cooked rice. Pound very thoroughly to a soft pulp; this can be done in a blender, in which case add the reserved liquid. If done by hand, add the reserved liquid after the pounding is completed. Add 1$\frac{1}{4}$ cups fish broth and strain. Add the remaining fish broth, pour the soup into a clean saucepan and reheat gently. Beat in the remaining butter in small pieces. Add the cream and season with salt and cayenne. Reheat, if necessary, without boiling. Serve hot, with warmed slices of French bread.

Above: Lobster bisque

Below: Tomato and celery soup

Tomato and celery soup

Serves 4

2 tablespoons butter
2 medium-sized onions, chopped
3–4 celery stalks
4 large tomatoes, peeled and chopped
1$\frac{1}{4}$ cups chicken broth
salt and pepper
1 tablespoon concentrated tomato paste
chopped celery leaves, to garnish

Melt the butter in a large saucepan and add the onions and celery; cook for a few minutes. Add tomatoes and broth and simmer for 15 minutes. Put the soup in a blender and purée or pass it through a strainer. Return it to the pan, heat for a few minutes, then add the seasoning and tomato paste. Pour into soup cups or a tureen. Garnish with celery leaves. This soup may also be served chilled.

Gazpacho
Serves 6

8 large tomatoes, peeled
½ cucumber, peeled and
finely diced
1 green pepper, seeded and diced
1 red pepper, seeded and diced
6 scallions, thinly sliced
1 tablespoon olive oil
1 tablespoon wine vinegar
1¼ cups chilled water
1 garlic clove, crushed
salt
freshly ground black pepper
finely chopped yolk of hard-boiled egg,
to garnish

Purée the tomatoes in a blender, or press through a strainer with a wooden spoon. Stir the prepared vegetables into the tomato purée with the olive oil, vinegar and chilled water. Add the crushed garlic and season with salt and pepper. Chill well. Serve the cold soup in chilled soup bowls. Sprinkle chopped egg yolk in the center of each portion and add an ice cube just before serving.

Above left: Gazpacho
Below left: Chicken chowder

Chicken chowder
Serves 4 to 6

2–3 bacon slices, chopped
1 medium-sized onion, chopped
2 cups chicken broth
1½ cups diced potatoes
1¼ cups milk
1 cup diced cooked chicken
¼ cup whole kernel corn
salt and pepper
chopped parsley, to garnish
paprika, to garnish

Cook the bacon in a large saucepan a few minutes, then add the onion and cook together until the bacon is crisp. Add the broth and bring to a boil. Add the potatoes and cook until they are just tender. Add the milk, chicken, whole kernel corn and seasoning. Simmer for a few minutes, then serve the chowder garnished with parsley and paprika.

Minestrone

Serves 6 to 8
This hearty soup, one of the world's classic dishes, originated in the area surrounding Italy's gastronomic capital – Bologna. The region is rich agriculturally and also recognized as the home of Italy's finest meat and dairy produce – including the vital ingredient of many popular Italian dishes, Parmesan cheese. Not surprisingly the flavor of this soup is greatly enhanced by freshly grated Parmesan cheese. It is worth buying a chunk from a delicatessen, rather than using already grated cheese.

Minestrone

3 tablespoons olive oil

2 large onions, thinly sliced

2 garlic cloves, crushed

2–3 bacon slices, chopped

4 tomatoes, peeled, seeded and chopped

$\frac{1}{2}$ cup navy beans, soaked overnight in water and drained

1 small glass red wine

$7\frac{1}{2}$ cups water

1 teaspoon finely chopped fresh marjoram

$\frac{1}{2}$ teaspoon finely chopped fresh thyme

2 carrots, pared and diced

2 potatoes, pared and diced

1 small turnip, diced

1–2 celery stalks, chopped

$\frac{1}{2}$ small head cabbage, shredded

$\frac{1}{2}$ cup elbow macaroni or pasta shells

1 tablespoon finely chopped parsley

salt and pepper

grated Parmesan cheese, to serve

Heat the oil in a large saucepan. Add the onions, garlic and bacon and cook gently for a few minutes. Add the tomatoes, beans and wine and cook for a few minutes more. Then add the water, marjoram and thyme, bring to a boil, cover and simmer about 2 hours or until the beans are tender.

Add the carrots and cook for about 10 minutes, then add the potatoes and turnip. Cook for a few more minutes, then add the celery, cabbage and pasta. Cook until the pasta and all the vegetables are tender, then add the parsley and season. Stir in 2 to 3 tablespoons grated Parmesan.

Salads

Mixed salad

Mixed salad
Serves 4 to 6

4 large tomatoes, thinly sliced
$\frac{1}{4}$ cucumber, sliced
1 green or red pepper, seeded and sliced
1 celery stalk, chopped
a few black olives, pitted and chopped
a few scallions, chopped
a few dill pickles, chopped
$\frac{1}{2}$ crisp head lettuce, shredded, or bunch of watercress
bottled soured cream dressing

Arrange all the ingredients on a large serving platter and dress with soured cream dressing just before serving.

Country garden salad
Serves 4

1 cup cooked sliced green beans
$\frac{1}{2}$ cup cooked or canned and drained whole kernel corn
$\frac{1}{2}$ red pepper, seeded, sliced and diced
$\frac{1}{2}$ cup sliced mushrooms
2 large tomatoes, thinly sliced
To garnish
black olives, pitted
1 small onion, sliced
bottle oil and vinegar dressing

Mix all the ingredients in a bowl and toss with the oil and vinegar dressing. Arrange on a large serving plate and garnish with black olives and thin slices of onion. Serve with cold chicken or turkey, or as a luncheon salad with warmed French bread.

Above: Country garden salad
Below: Hawaiian salad plate

Hawaiian salad plate

Serves 4
This salad is also delicious with more exotic tropical fruit, such as mangoes and papayas.

1 small head Boston lettuce
1–2 heads French or Belgian endive
1 apple, cored and sliced
bottled oil and vinegar dressing
1 cup cottage cheese
fresh or canned pineapple rings, drained
2–3 oranges, peeled and divided into segments
$\frac{1}{4}$ cucumber, sliced

Arrange washed lettuce leaves on a large flat dish. Wash and separate endive leaves and decoratively arrange them at each end of the dish. Dip the apple slices in the bottled oil and vinegar dressing to prevent discoloration. Spoon the cottage cheese in the center of the lettuce and garnish with the pineapple rings, orange segments and apple and cucumber slices.

23

Pasta slaw

Carrot and apple salad

Pasta slaw
Serves 6

1 cup elbow macaroni

salt and pepper

½ small head white cabbage, shredded

1 small green pepper, seeded, sliced and diced

3 tomatoes, quartered and thinly sliced

For the dressing

¼ cup thick mayonnaise

1 tablespoon dairy soured cream

1 tablespoon vinegar

2 teaspoons sugar

Cook the pasta in boiling salted water for 10–12 minutes, or until tender. Drain, rinse in cold water and drain again. Mix together ingredients for the dressing and stir in pasta and other ingredients. Place in a bowl and arrange tomato slices on top.

Carrot and apple salad

Top prepared lettuce and watercress or other green salad vegetables with coarsely grated carrot, as shown in the picture. Arrange segments of apple, dipped in oil and vinegar dressing, as a garnish. If wished, finely chopped apple and nuts may be mixed with the carrot. Serve with cooked sausages, pork, goose or other fairly rich meats.

Chicken-peach salad

Arrange prepared lettuce, watercress and Belgian endive in a bowl. Top with neatly diced pieces of cold, cooked chicken, sliced fresh pear, dipped in oil and vinegar dressing, sliced canned peaches and fresh or dried dates. Serve with mayonnaise or oil and vinegar dressing and garnish with lemon slices.

Chicken peach salad

Tomato and orange salad

Serves 4 to 6

6 tomatoes, cut into wedges

2 oranges, peeled and segmented

1 tablespoon finely chopped fresh basil, or 1 teaspoon dried basil finely grated rind of 1 lemon

For the dressing

3 tablespoons olive oil

3 tablespoons orange juice

$\frac{1}{2}$ teaspoon superfine sugar

salt and pepper

Decoratively arrange the tomatoes and orange segments in a serving dish. Sprinkle them with basil and lemon rind. Mix together all the dressing ingredients and pour over the oranges and tomatoes. Chill at least 30 minutes.

Serve with cold meat, cold fish salads or barbecued meat. This also makes a summer lunch salad served with cottage cheese.

Above: Tomato and orange salad
Right: Citrus green salad

Citrus green salad

Serves 4 to 6

1 head Iceberg lettuce, shredded

1 bunch watercress, washed and picked over

2 large grapefruit, peeled and divided into segments

2 large oranges, peeled and divided into segments

bottled oil and vinegar dressing

Mix all ingredients together in a salad bowl and toss gently in the oil and vinegar dressing. Serve immediately.

Cracked wheat salad

Cracked wheat salad
Serves 8

$\frac{1}{2}$ lb cracked wheat, soaked in water for 30 minutes
6 scallions, finely chopped
sea salt
freshly ground black pepper
$1\frac{1}{4}$ cups finely chopped fresh parsley
$1\frac{1}{4}$ cups finely chopped fresh mint
2 tablespoons olive oil
2 tablespoons lemon juice
For the garnish
cucumber slices
black olives, pitted

Drain the cracked wheat and wrap it in a clean dry towel to squeeze out as much moisture as possible. Spread it out to dry further. Mix the wheat with the chopped scallions, crushing them so that their juices soak into the wheat. Season with salt and pepper. Add the parsley, mint, olive oil and lemon juice and mix well. Taste, and adjust the seasoning. The salad should have a distinctive lemon taste. Garnish with cucumber slices and black olives. If wished, add some tomato slices, strips of green pepper and sprigs of parsley.

Above: Summer salad; Right: Orange and endive salad and Celery, apple and beet salad

Summer salad
Serves 4

1 cup elbow macaroni
salt and pepper
lemon juice
1 can (7 oz) tuna, drained and flaked
$\frac{1}{4}$ cup raisins
$\frac{1}{4}$ cup finely chopped walnuts
2 celery stalks, chopped
3 tablespoons thick mayonnaise
few lettuce leaves
finely chopped fresh chives
To garnish
1 apple, cored and sliced
celery leaves, to garnish

Cook macaroni in boiling salted water until tender. Drain, rinse in cold water and drain again. Dip a few apple slices in lemon juice to prevent discoloration. Place tuna in a bowl. Add the raisins, nuts, remaining apple, celery and mayonnaise. Season to taste and mix well.

Line a dish with the lettuce leaves and pile the salad into the center. Sprinkle with chopped chives. Garnish with the reserved apple slices and celery leaves.

Celery, apple and beet salad
Serves 2

4 celery stalks
1 apple
1 medium-sized cooked beet
$\frac{1}{4}$ teaspoon salt
1 tablespoon lemon juice

Wash and chop the celery. Pare, core and slice the apple and chop the beet. Mix with the other ingredients and serve immediately.

Orange and endive salad
Serves 2

1 orange
1 large head Belgian endive
parsley sprigs
For the dressing
1 tablespoon oil
$\frac{1}{2}$ teaspoon sugar
$\frac{1}{4}$ teaspoon salt
1 tablespoon lemon juice

Peel the orange and remove all the pith. Cut the orange into very thin slices. Remove any tough outer leaves of the endive and trim off the bottom. Wash and dry the leaves. Arrange the endive and orange slices on a shallow dish. Mix the dressing ingredients well and pour the dressing over the salad. Decorate with the parsley.

27

Vegetable dishes

Leeks mornay
Serves 4

8 leeks
salt and pepper
2 tablespoons butter
¼ cup all-purpose flour
pinch of mustard powder
1¼ cups milk, or half milk and half cooking liquid from leeks
1 cup grated cheese
paprika

Cook the leeks in boiling salted water for 10–20 minutes, or until tender. Drain and reserve ¾ cup of the liquid if needed for the sauce. Put the leeks on a heated serving dish and keep warm.

Melt the butter in a pan, stir in the flour and mustard powder and cook for 1–2 minutes. Gradually blend in the milk or milk and cooking liquid, stirring all the time, and bring to a boil. Turn down the heat, stir in the cheese and add seasoning. Pour the sauce over the leeks and sprinkle with paprika.

Mediterranean stuffed tomatoes
Serves 8

4 large tomatoes
⅔ cup fresh white bread crumbs
1 medium-sized onion, finely chopped
1 garlic clove, crushed
½ cup finely chopped mushrooms
8 blanched almonds, finely chopped
1 tablespoon chopped parsley
salt and pepper
2 tablespoons butter
8 black olives, to garnish

Preheat oven to 350°. Cut the tomatoes in half, scoop out the middle part and reserve. Turn the tomato shells upside down to drain. Strain the seeds from the reserved tomato and blend the pulp with the bread crumbs, onion, garlic, mushrooms, almonds, parsley and seasoning. Pile the mixture into the tomato shells. Put a small knob of butter on top of each tomato and place in an ovenproof dish. Bake 15–20 minutes, or until golden brown. Garnish each tomato with an olive before serving.

Opposite left: Leeks mornay
Opposite right: Mediterranean
stuffed tomatoes
Below: Stuffed eggplant
Right: Potatoes with cheese

Stuffed eggplant
Serves 4

2 medium-sized eggplant
salt and pepper
olive oil
1 cup fresh white bread crumbs
2 hard-boiled eggs, chopped
8 green olives, pitted and sliced
1 small garlic clove, crushed
8 anchovy fillets, chopped
squeeze of lemon juice
1 tablespoon chopped parsley
1 teaspoon dried marjoram
parsley sprigs, to garnish

Preheat oven to 350°. Cut the eggplant in half lengthwise. Make gashes in the flesh and stand them, cut side up, in an oiled baking pan. Sprinkle with salt and pepper and brush fairly thickly with olive oil. Cook 30 minutes. Remove from oven and leave to cool slightly. Carefully cut out the flesh, leaving an eggplant shell of $\frac{1}{4}$ inch. Chop the flesh finely and put it in a bowl. Add the remaining ingredients and season, taking into account the saltiness of the anchovies. Put the mixture in the eggplant shells and sprinkle lightly with olive oil. Cook in the center of the oven 30 minutes. Serve garnished with parsley sprigs.

Potatoes with cheese
Serves 4

4 large potatoes, thinly sliced
$1\frac{1}{4}$ cups, chicken broth
1 egg, beaten
salt and pepper
$\frac{1}{4}$ teaspoon ground nutmeg
$\frac{1}{2}$ cup grated Swiss cheese
1 garlic clove, halved
2 tablespoons butter

Preheat oven to 325°. Put the potatoes in a bowl and add the broth with the egg beaten into it. Season with salt, pepper and nutmeg. Add the grated cheese and mix thoroughly.

Grease an ovenproof dish and rub it with the cut garlic clove. Add the potato mixture and dot with small pieces of butter. Cook 40–50 minutes, or until the potato is cooked and the top is beginning to brown.

French-fried fennel

Ratatouille
Serves 6 to 8

1 medium to large eggplant, sliced and sprinkled with salt
½ lb zucchini, sliced and sprinkled with salt
¼ cup olive oil
2 large tomatoes, peeled
2 medium-sized onions, peeled and sliced
1–2 garlic cloves, crushed
1 green pepper, seeded and cut into strips
1 red pepper, seeded and cut into strips
salt and pepper
freshly chopped parsley, to garnish

Leave the salted eggplant and zucchini slices for about 30 minutes. Then wipe away excess moisture to remove any bitterness.

Heat the olive oil in a saucepan, add the tomatoes and onions and cook gently for a few minutes. Add the rest of the vegetables and stir well. Season and cover the pan with a tightly fitting lid. Simmer gently for about 30 minutes. Garnish with chopped parsley if wished. Ratatouille may be served hot or chilled.

French-fried fennel
Serves 4

1 Florentine fennel
½ cup all-purpose flour
salt
1 egg, beaten
6 tablespoons milk
oil or fat, for frying

Wash the fennel and remove the green leaves, reserving some for garnish. Slice and separate into rings.

Sift the flour into a bowl with a pinch of salt. Make a well in the middle, drop in the egg and gradually mix in the flour. Beat in the milk to make a smooth batter.

Heat the oil or fat in a deep saucepan. Coat the fennel rings in the batter and fry 2–3 minutes, until the batter is crisp. Garnish with the reserved fennel leaves.

Above: Ratatouille
Right: Red cabbage (recipe overleaf)

Red cabbage

Serves 4

1 medium-sized red cabbage, finely shredded
1 lb cooking apples, pared, cored and sliced
¾ cup water
3 tablespoons sugar
1 teaspoon salt
4 cloves
¼ cup vinegar
¼ cup (½ stick) butter
1 tablespoon red currant jelly

Put the cabbage and apples in a saucepan with the water, sugar, salt, cloves and vinegar. Cover and simmer for 1½–2 hours. Just before the end of the cooking time, stir in the butter and red currant jelly. Serve hot.

Red peppers

Serves 4

3 tablespoons olive oil
1 tablespoon butter
1 small onion, finely chopped
½ garlic clove, crushed
4 red peppers, seeded and cut into strips
salt and pepper
4–5 tomatoes, peeled and quartered
chopped parsley, to garnish

Heat the oil and butter in a saucepan, add the onion and garlic and cook until the onion is soft and transparent. Add the peppers and season, cover and cook gently for 15 minutes.

Add the tomatoes, cover, and cook over low heat for about 30 minutes. Garnish with chopped parsley before serving.

Above: Red peppers
Right: Broccoli polonaise (top), Carrots and fried almonds (below left) and Peas and cucumber (below right)

Broccoli polonaise

Serves 4

1 lb fresh or frozen broccoli spears
salt
½ cup (1 stick) butter
1 cup fresh white bread crumbs
2 hard-boiled eggs, whites finely chopped and yolks strained
2 tablespoons chopped parsley

Cook the broccoli in boiling salted water for 5 minutes if frozen and 20 minutes if fresh. Drain well, put in a heated serving dish and add one-third of the butter. Set aside and keep hot.

Fry the bread crumbs in the remaining butter until they are crisp and golden. Sprinkle them over the broccoli. Arrange a circle of egg white around the edge of the dish, then a circle of egg yolk and then a circle of parsley.

Peas and cucumber
Serves 4

1 medium cucumber, peeled and diced
2 tablespoons butter
½ lb frozen peas, or fresh hulled peas
salt

Cook the cucumber gently in the butter, stirring frequently, until it is pale golden. Meanwhile, cook the peas in boiling salted water for 5 minutes, or 15–20 minutes for fresh peas. Drain the peas and mix with the cucumber.

Carrots and fried almonds
Serves 4

1 lb carrots, sliced
salt
½ cup blanched almonds
2 tablespoons butter

Put the carrot slices in a pan with just enough salted water to cover. Cook, tightly covered, for 10–15 minutes. Meanwhile cook the almonds in the butter, stirring, until they are golden brown. Finish cooking the carrots with the lid off until all the water has cooked away. Then mix the carrots with almonds and butter.

33

Boston baked beans

Serves 6 to 8
Early New England settlers were fond of large pots of Boston baked beans. Economical and filling, this dish was not only ideal for facing the harsh winters but also its preparation was suitable for the strict religious practices. The cooking was usually begun on Friday night or Saturday morning so the beans would be tender by Saturday evening when all work had to stop as part of the Sunday observances.

1 lb dried navy or lima beans, soaked overnight and drained
2 large tomatoes, peeled and chopped
1–2 tablespoons molasses
1–2 teaspoons mustard
salt and pepper
$\frac{3}{4}$ lb fat salt pork or 6 bacon slices, diced
1–2 medium-sized onions, thinly sliced
parsley, to garnish

Boston baked beans

Put the beans in a saucepan with water to cover and simmer for 10–15 minutes. Strain the beans but reserve $1\frac{1}{4}$ cups of the liquid. Simmer the tomatoes in this liquid to make a sauce, then strain. Add molasses, mustard and a generous amount of salt and pepper to the tomato sauce. Put the beans, pork or bacon and onions in a deep ovenproof dish, pour over the tomato sauce and mix well. Make sure there is plenty of space on top for the beans to swell during cooking.

Preheat oven to 260°. Cover the dish tightly; if the lid does not fit well, cover with foil before putting the lid on. Cook in the center of the oven. After $2\frac{1}{2}$ hours, check the progress of the cooking. If the beans are still hard, raise the temperature slightly. If they are becoming a little dry, add enough boiling water to moisten, but do not make them too wet. Continue cooking until beans are tender, about another $3\frac{1}{2}$ hours. Top with parsley before serving.

Cheese and potato ring

Serves 4 to 6

4 large potatoes
3 medium-sized onions
$\frac{1}{4}$ cup ($\frac{1}{2}$ stick) butter
$1\frac{1}{2}$ cups coarsely grated cheese
salt and pepper
paprika
parsley sprigs, to garnish

Preheat oven to 350°. Grate the potatoes and onions very coarsely or cut them into small, thin strips. Melt the butter in a saucepan and toss the vegetables in it with half the cheese and plenty of salt, pepper and paprika. Put a well-greased ring mold 8 inches in diameter in the preheated oven. When the mold is very hot, remove it from the oven and press the potato mixture into it, pressing down well. Cover with greased foil and bake 45 minutes. Turn out carefully onto a heated ovenproof dish. Spoon the rest of the cheese over the ring at intervals and return it to the oven for 5–10 minutes, or until the cheese has melted. Garnish the ring with parsley sprigs.

Cauliflower with brown sauce topping

Serves 4

1 cauliflower
pinch of salt
chopped parsley
For the brown sauce
tomato juice
2 tablespoons butter
¼ cup all-purpose flour
little yeast extract

Cut the cauliflower into flowerets and cook in about 3 inches boiling salted water for 10–15 minutes, or until just tender. Drain and reserve the liquid for the sauce. Keep the cauliflower hot.

To make the sauce, measure the cooking liquid and make it up to 1¼ cups with tomato juice. Melt the butter in a pan, stir in the flour and cook gently for 2 minutes. Gradually stir in the liquid, bring to a boil and stir until the sauce thickens. Add enough yeast extract to give a fairly pronounced flavor. Put the cauliflower in a serving dish and pour the sauce over. Sprinkle with parsley.

Right: Cauliflower with brown sauce topping
Below: Cheese and potato ring

Egg dishes

Bornholm omelet
Serves 4 to 6

6–8 eggs
2 tablespoons light cream or milk
salt and pepper
$\frac{1}{4}$ cup ($\frac{1}{2}$ stick) butter
3 herring fillets, cut into strips
few radishes, sliced
few lettuce leaves, shredded
2 tablespoons chopped chives or scallions

Beat the eggs with the cream or milk, and seasoning.
Melt the butter in a large omelet pan, pour in the
eggs and cook rapidly, stirring with a fork. Bring
some of the cooked mixture to the center, allowing
the uncooked egg to come into contact with the pan.
When the egg is just set and the underside is a light
golden brown, slide the omelet (without folding) onto
a heated serving dish. Top with the herring pieces,
radish slices, shredded lettuce and the chives or
scallions.

Cheese soufflé
Serves 4

2 tablespoons butter
$\frac{1}{4}$ cup all-purpose flour
$\frac{1}{2}$ cup milk
$\frac{1}{2}$ teaspoon salt
pinch of cayenne
$\frac{1}{4}$ teaspoon mustard powder
4 eggs, separated
$\frac{3}{4}$ cup grated sharp Cheddar cheese

Preheat oven to 375°. Melt the butter in a large
saucepan, stir in the flour and cook for a minute or
two. Gradually blend in the milk, stirring all the time
with a wooden spoon. Cook until the sauce is thick,
then add the seasonings. Remove from the heat and
add the egg yolks, then the cheese. Beat the egg
whites until stiff, then fold them into the mixture.
Put the mixture in a greased soufflé dish and cook in
center of oven for about 30 minutes. Serve
immediately.

Right: Bornholm omelet
Far right: Cheese soufflé

Scotch eggs

Pipérade

Scotch eggs
Serves 4

| 4 hard-boiled eggs |
| little flour |
| salt and pepper |
| ¾ lb sausage meat |
| 1 egg, beaten |
| 3 tablespoons dry bread crumbs |
| deep fat or oil for frying |

When the eggs are cool, coat each one in a little seasoned flour. Divide the sausage meat into four equal portions and press them out into squares on a floured board. Wrap a square of sausage meat around each egg, seal the edges and roll into a neat shape. Coat the eggs in beaten egg and crumbs. Deep fry the eggs until they are golden brown. Cool them, then cut in half to serve.

Pipérade
Serves 4

| ¼ cup (½ stick) butter |
| 1 green pepper and 1 red pepper, each seeded, sliced and diced |
| 1 small onion, finely chopped |
| 2 tomatoes, peeled and chopped |
| 1 garlic clove, crushed |
| 6 eggs, beaten |
| salt and pepper |

Melt the butter in a heavy skillet. Add the peppers, onion, tomatoes and garlic. Cook gently until tender, then add the seasoned beaten eggs and stir with a wooden spoon until the eggs are just set. Serve with French bread or hot buttered toast.

Cheese omelet

Cheese omelet
Serves 1

| 2 eggs |
| 1 tablespoon water |
| salt and pepper |
| 1 tablespoon butter |
| ¼ cup grated sharp Cheddar cheese |

Beat the eggs lightly with a fork until the whites and yolks are mixed but not frothy. Stir in the water and seasoning.

Melt the butter in an omelet pan. Add the egg mixture and cook rapidly, stirring with a fork. Bring some of the cooked mixture to the center, allowing the uncooked egg to come into contact with the pan. When the top is almost set add the grated cheese. When the cheese is melted and the underside of the omelet is a light golden brown, fold the omelet and turn it onto a heated plate. Serve immediately.

Omelet cake

Serves 4 to 5

8 eggs
salt and pepper
3 tablespoons water
$\frac{1}{4}$ cup ($\frac{1}{2}$ stick) butter
For the sauce
6 tomatoes, peeled and chopped
$\frac{1}{8}$ lb ground beef
1 garlic clove, crushed
1 onion, chopped
salt and pepper
pinch of dried or fresh basil
Layer one
1 cup cooked mixed vegetables
little butter
Layer two
1 cup chopped mushrooms
$\frac{1}{4}$ cup ($\frac{1}{2}$ stick) butter
Layer three
1 cup deveined cooked shrimp
little butter

First make the sauce: Simmer the tomatoes in a saucepan until the juice flows. Then add the beef, garlic, onion, seasoning and herbs. Simmer for about 30 minutes, then strain if wished. Keep hot.

Heat the mixed vegetables in the minimum of butter. Cook mushrooms in butter. Toss the shrimp in butter.

Beat the eggs with the seasoning and water. Make four omelets, cooking each one as follows: heat a quarter of the butter in an omelet pan and add a quarter of the egg mixture. Cook rapidly, stirring with a fork and bring the cooked mixture to the center so that the uncooked egg comes into contact with the pan. Cook until the egg is set and the bottom is a light golden brown. Put the first omelet on a hot serving dish. Cover it with the vegetable layer, then add the second omelet and the mushrooms, then the third omelet and the shrimp. Put the fourth omelet on top and spoon over some of the sauce. Serve the rest of the sauce separately.

Above: Omelet cake
Below: Scrambled eggs

Scrambled eggs

Serves 2

4 eggs
salt and pepper
2 tablespoons milk or light cream
2 tablespoons butter
To garnish
paprika
1 tablespoon chopped parsley

Beat the eggs with seasoning and milk or cream. Melt the butter in a saucepan over low heat. Pour in the eggs and stir lightly with a wooden spoon until just set.

Serve with hot buttered toast. For a light meal, serve with creamed potatoes piped around the edge and sprinkle with paprika and chopped parsley.

Chilled cheese soufflé

Eggs au gratin
Serves 2

2 tablespoons butter
¼ cup all-purpose flour
1¼ cups milk
salt and pepper
1 cup grated sharp Cheddar cheese
4 eggs, hard-boiled and shelled
Topping
2 tablespoons grated sharp Cheddar cheese
2 tablespoons dry bread crumbs

Melt the butter in a pan, stir in the flour and cook for 1 minute. Gradually blend in the milk, stirring constantly, until the sauce thickens. Season well and stir in the cheese; cook gently until the cheese has melted.

Arrange the whole eggs in a heatproof dish and pour over the sauce. Sprinkle the grated cheese and bread crumbs on top and brown under the broiler or in a hot oven.

Chilled cheese soufflé
Serves 6 to 8

1 envelope unflavored gelatin
1¼ cups very hot water
3 eggs, separated
½ cup heavy cream
¾ cup light cream
1 cup finely grated Cheddar or Swiss cheese
salt and pepper
To garnish
dill pickles, cut in fans
tomatoes, sliced

Cut a piece of waxed paper three times the depth of the dish. Fold the paper in half to give a double thickness and tie it around the dish. Brush the part that stands above the dish with melted butter.

Dissolve the gelatin in 1 tablespoon hot water. Beat it into the egg yolks and continue beating until it is well blended. Leave it to cool. Meanwhile, beat the heavy cream until it holds its shape, then gradually beat in the light cream, cheese and seasoning.

Fold the gelatin and egg yolks into the cream mixture. Beat the egg whites until stiff and fold them in. Spoon the mixture into the prepared soufflé dish and leave to set.

Remove the paper from the dish and garnish with dill pickle fans and tomato slices.

Soufflé omelet
Serves 1

2 or 3 eggs
salt and pepper
1 tablespoon water
2 tablespoons butter
For the filling
½ cup cooked mixed vegetables
5 tablespoons catsup, or concentrated tomato paste

Separate the egg yolks from the whites. Beat the yolks with seasoning and water. Beat the egg whites until very stiff, then fold them into the yolks. Preheat the broiler. Mix the vegetables with the catsup or paste and put over gentle heat. Melt the butter in an omelet pan until it is frothy. Pour the egg mixture in, let it set for a few seconds, then stir with a fork. Draw the cooked mixture to the center of the pan and let the uncooked egg come into contact with the pan. When the omelet is half cooked, put the pan under the broiler to complete the cooking. Make a shallow cut across the middle of the omelet so that it will fold easily, then spoon on the filling. Fold the omelet and serve.

Opposite top: Eggs au gratin
Opposite bottom: Soufflé omelet

Rice, pasta & pizzas

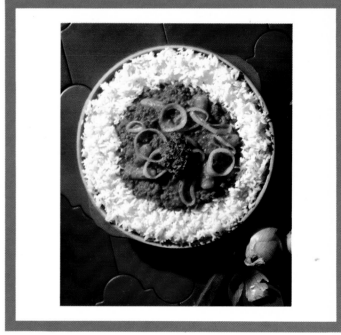

Chicken pilaf
Serves 4 to 5

2 tablespoons vegetable oil
2 medium-sized onions, chopped
1 garlic clove, crushed
1¼ cups long grain rice
2½ cups chicken broth
½ cup golden raisins
few pine nuts, cashews or other nuts (optional)
2 cups diced cooked chicken
salt and pepper
extra nuts, to garnish

Heat the oil in a large skillet and cook the onions and garlic for a few minutes. Then add the rice, turning it in the oil so that all the grains are separate. Add the broth, bring to a boil and stir, then simmer in the uncovered skillet for about 10 minutes. Add the rest of the ingredients and cook for 10–15 minutes more, until the liquid has been absorbed. Pile on to a hot serving dish and sprinkle with extra nuts.

Beef risotto Milanaise

Serves 4

2 tablespoons oil

2 medium-sized onions, thinly sliced

1–2 garlic cloves, thinly sliced

1 lb ground beef

1 can (about 8 oz) tomatoes

4 carrots, chopped

1 tablespoon concentrated tomato paste

salt and pepper

1 bay leaf

1¼ cups long grain rice

2½ cups water

parsley sprig, to garnish

Heat the oil in a large saucepan and cook the onions and garlic until the onions are transparent. Put a few rings of onion aside for the garnish. Add the beef to the pan, stirring well to break up any lumps. Add the tomatoes and liquid from the can, the carrots, tomato paste, seasoning and bay leaf. Cover the pan and cook gently for 45 minutes, stirring once or twice.

Put the rice and cold water in a pan with ½–1 teaspoon salt. Bring water to a boil, stir briskly, then cover. Lower the heat and cook for about 15 minutes, until the rice is tender and the liquid is absorbed. Fork the rice onto a hot dish. Spoon the beef mixture in the center and garnish with the reserved onion rings and the sprig of parsley.

Risotto

Serves 4

¼ cup (½ stick) butter

1 medium-sized onion, finely chopped

1 garlic clove, crushed

1¼ cups long grain rice

2½ cups chicken broth

few strands of saffron

salt and pepper

little ground nutmeg

1 tablespoon concentrated tomato paste

grated Parmesan cheese

watercress sprig, to garnish

Melt the butter in a large skillet. Add the onion and garlic and cook gently until the onion is transparent. Then add the rice and turn it in the butter until every grain is separate. Blend a little of the broth with the saffron. Add the rest of the broth to the pan with the salt, pepper, nutmeg and tomato paste. Strain the saffron-infused broth and add it to the pan. Stir well. Cook gently until the rice has absorbed the liquid, stirring occasionally. Top with the grated cheese and serve, garnished with the watercress.

Variations: The risotto can be varied, or made into a main dish, by adding a sliced hard-boiled egg, cooked or canned pimientos, chicken livers cooked in butter or shrimp.

Opposite far left: Chicken pilaf
Opposite above: Beef risotto milanaise
Right: Risotto

Fried rice with ham and bean sprouts

Serves 6 to 8

2 tablespoons vegetable oil
2 scallions, finely chopped
1 garlic clove, crushed
6 cups cooked rice
1 cup chopped ham
2 tablespoons soy sauce
2 eggs, beaten
salt and pepper
½ lb canned bean sprouts, drained

Heat the oil in a skillet or wok and fry the scallions and garlic for 2 minutes over medium heat. Add the rice, mix well and heat through. Mix the ham with the soy sauce, add it to the rice mixture and mix well. Season the beaten eggs with salt and pepper, and pour into the rice in a thin stream, stirring constantly, until the eggs are cooked. Stir in the bean sprouts and heat through. Serve immediately.

Noodle ring with meat sauce

Serves 4

2 tablespoons oil
1 onion, chopped
1 garlic clove, crushed
½ lb ground beef
1 tablespoon concentrated tomato paste
1 green apple, cored and chopped
salt and pepper
¼ teaspoon sugar
¼ teaspoon dried basil
1 can (about 8 oz) tomatoes
¾ lb ribbon noodles
finely chopped fresh parsley

Heat the oil in a saucepan and cook the onion and garlic until the onion begins to brown. Add the meat and stir over medium heat for about 5 minutes, until the meat is browned. Add the tomato paste, apple, salt, pepper, sugar, basil and tomatoes. Cover the pan and simmer for about 40 minutes. While the sauce is cooking, cook the noodles in boiling, salted water for about 12 minutes, or according to the directions on the package. Pack the cooked noodles into a buttered ring mold and keep hot.

When the sauce is ready, turn the noodle ring onto a hot serving dish, pile the sauce in the middle, and sprinkle with chopped parsley. Garnish with some extra chopped apple.

Spaghetti with tomato and anchovy sauce
Serves 4

2 tablespoons olive oil
2 garlic cloves, chopped
8 large tomatoes, peeled and chopped
6–8 anchovy fillets, chopped
2 teaspoons finely chopped mint, or 1 tablespoon chopped parsley
1 tablespoon chopped basil
salt and pepper
¾ lb spaghetti
butter
grated Parmesan cheese, to serve

Heat the olive oil with the garlic, then add the tomatoes and anchovy fillets. Cook for 10 minutes, then add the herbs and season well. Simmer gently for a few more minutes.

While the sauce is cooking, cook the spaghetti in boiling salted water for about 12 minutes, or according to directions on the the package. Drain and toss in butter. Pour the sauce over the top and serve with grated Parmesan cheese.

Opposite left: Fried rice with ham and bean sprouts; Left: Spaghetti with tomato and anchovy sauce; Below: Noodle ring with meat sauce

Spaghetti Bolognese
Serves 4

$\frac{3}{4}$ lb spaghetti

salt

butter

grated Parmesan cheese

For the Bolognese sauce

2 tablespoons butter

3 bacon slices, chopped

1 large onion, finely chopped

1 carrot, pared and chopped

1 celery stalk, finely chopped

$\frac{1}{2}$ lb lean ground beef

1 cup chopped chicken liver

1 tablespoon concentrated tomato paste

$\frac{1}{3}$ cup white wine

$1\frac{1}{4}$ cups broth or water

salt and pepper

ground nutmeg

$\frac{1}{4}$ cup light cream or milk

First make the sauce: Melt the butter in a saucepan and cook the bacon, onion, carrot and celery for about 10 minutes, or until the vegetables are soft. Add the meat; when it has browned, add the chopped chicken livers. Cook for 2–3 minutes, then add the tomato paste, wine and broth or water. Add salt and pepper and ground nutmeg. Stir the sauce until it boils, then reduce the heat, cover and simmer for about 40 minutes, stirring occasionally. Just before serving, stir in the cream or milk and check to see if it needs more seasoning.

While the sauce is cooking, cook the spaghetti in boiling salted water for about 12 minutes, or according to the directions on the package. Drain the spaghetti, put it on a hot serving dish and put a generous amount of butter on top. Pour the sauce over and serve immediately with grated Parmesan cheese.

Above left: Spaghetti Bolognese
Above centre: Spaghetti with tomato sauce and olives
Above right: Lasagne

Spaghetti with tomato sauce and olives
Serves 4

¾ lb spaghetti
salt
12–16 large black olives, pitted and halved
2 tablespoons olive oil
butter
1 jar (8 oz) tomato sauce, hot
grated Parmesan cheese

Cook the spaghetti in boiling salted water for about 12 minutes, or according to package directions. Cook the olives for 2–3 minutes in a little olive oil.

Drain the spaghetti, put it on a hot serving dish and put a generous amount of butter on top. Pour the tomato sauce over and arrange the olives on top. Serve immediately with grated Parmesan cheese.

Lasagne
Serves 4

½ lb lasagne
Bolognese sauce (see recipe for Spaghetti Bolognese)
grated Parmesan cheese
butter
For the cheese sauce
¼ cup (½ stick) butter
3 tablespoons all-purpose flour
2 cups milk
½ cup grated Parmesan cheese
salt and pepper
pinch of ground nutmeg

Cook the lasagne in boiling salted water for 10–15 minutes, or according to package directions. Drain thoroughly and place each piece on paper towels to absorb moisture.

Make the cheese sauce: Melt the butter in a saucepan and stir in the flour. Cook 2 minutes, then blend in the milk. Bring to a boil, stirring constantly, until the sauce thickens. Stir in the cheese. Season with salt and pepper and nutmeg.

Preheat oven to 350°. Butter a deep ovenproof dish. Cover the base with Bolognese sauce, then add a layer of cheese sauce followed by a layer of lasagne. Repeat the layers and top with cheese sauce. Sprinkle thickly with cheese and dot with butter. Cook 30 minutes in the center of the oven. Serve immediately.

Pizza with olives and herbs

Serves 4 to 6

One of the reasons for pizza's popularity is its great versatility. It's perfect for parties and informal gatherings, without breaking the budget! This quick-and-easy recipe uses prepared pastry sticks for the base and olives for the topping. Yet the combinations of delicious and varied toppings are endless.

2 sticks (11 oz package) pie crust pastry
3 tablespoons olive oil
2 large onions, finely chopped
1 large garlic clove, crushed
1 large can (about 2½ lb) Italian tomatoes
2 tablespoons concentrated tomato paste
2 teaspoons dried oregano
2 teaspoons chopped fresh basil, or 1 teaspoon dried basil
1 bay leaf
2 teaspoons sugar
1 teaspoon salt
freshly ground black pepper
fresh herbs, as available
pitted green olives

Preheat oven to 375°. Roll out the dough and line an 8-inch fluted tart ring. Place some waxed paper over the pastry and put some dry beans in it. Bake 15 minutes.

Make the filling: Heat the oil in a saucepan and cook the onion and garlic until the onion is soft and transparent but not colored. Add the tomatoes, coarsely chopped, with the liquid from the can. Then add the tomato paste, oregano, basil, bay leaf, sugar, salt and pepper. Bring to a boil, lower the heat and simmer gently, uncovered, about 45 minutes, stirring occasionally. Remove the bay leaf, add more seasoning if necessary and pour the mixture into the pastry shell.

Sprinkle with coarsely chopped fresh herbs and a few drops of oil. Arrange the olives on top and bake 10 to 15 minutes, or until the pastry is golden brown.

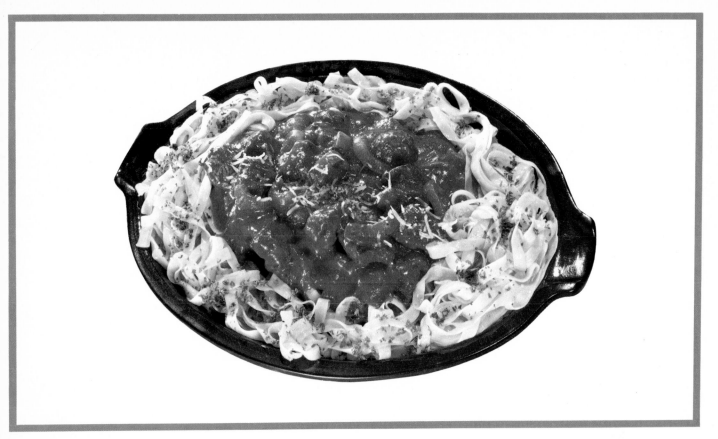

Opposite above: Pizza with olives and herbs; Opposite below: Mexican macaroni; Tagliatelle with liver sauce

Mexican macaroni
Serves 4

1 cup elbow macaroni
salt
8 frankfurters, chopped
1 cup cooked fresh peas
For the sauce
2 tablespoons butter
$\frac{1}{4}$ cup all-purpose flour
$1\frac{1}{4}$ cups milk
1 cup grated Cheddar cheese
salt and pepper
1 teaspoon mustard
pinch of cayenne

Cook the macaroni in boiling salted water according to the package directions.

While the macaroni is cooking, make the sauce: Melt the butter in a saucepan, add the flour and cook for 2 minutes, stirring. Blend in the milk and bring to a boil, stirring continually. When the sauce has thickened, reduce the heat and stir in the cheese and seasonings.

Drain the macaroni and add it to the sauce. Add the frankfurters with the peas. Heat for a few minutes and serve.

Tagliatelle with liver sauce
Serves 4

$\frac{1}{2}$ lb chicken livers
2 tablespoons all-purpose flour
2 tablespoons butter
1 tablespoon olive oil
1 small onion, finely chopped
1 garlic clove, chopped
1 cup sliced mushrooms
$\frac{3}{4}$ cup chicken broth
$\frac{1}{2}$ cup dry white wine
salt and pepper
$\frac{3}{4}$ lb tagliatelle or ribbon noodles
butter

First make the sauce: Cut the chicken livers into small pieces and coat with flour. Heat the butter and oil together in a saucepan. Add the onion and garlic and cook gently until pale gold. Add the liver and mushrooms. Cook more briskly for 3 to 4 minutes, stirring constantly. Add the broth and wine and season. Bring to a boil, stirring, then lower the heat and cover the pan. Simmer gently for 15 minutes.

While the sauce is cooking, cook the tagliatelle in boiling salted water for about 12 minutes, or according to package directions. Put the tagliatelle on a heated serving dish and put a generous amount of butter on top. Pour the sauce over and serve immediately.

Stuffed lasagne
Serves 4

The secret of good pasta is in the cooking – it should be neither too crunchy nor too mushy. The Italians describe the perfectly cooked pasta as al dente, *meaning just firm to the bite. Bring the water to a roaring boil and add the lasagne one piece at a time so the water never stops boiling. The tablespoon of vegetable oil prevents the lasagne, or any other pasta shapes, from sticking together.*

8 pieces of wide lasagne
1¼ cups cheese sauce (see recipe for Lasagne)
For the filling
1 bacon slice, cut into small pieces
1 small onion, chopped
½ lb lean ground beef
1 tablespoon vegetable or corn oil
1 celery stalk, chopped
½ garlic clove, crushed
¼ teaspoon dried mixed herbs
salt and pepper
pinch of sugar
3 tablespoons concentrated tomato paste
¾ cup water

First make the filling: Cook the bacon, onion and beef in the oil until brown, stirring frequently. Add all the remaining filling ingredients and stir well. Cover and simmer for 1 hour.

Cook the lasagne in boiling salted water with 1 tablespoon of vegetable oil added for 8–10 minutes, or according to package directions. When it is tender, drain, rinse and drain again. Arrange the pieces of pasta on a damp dish towel so that they do not stick together. Place a spoonful of the filling on each piece of lasagne and roll up. Put the lasagne rolls in a greased ovenproof dish.

Preheat oven to 350°. Pour the cheese sauce over the rolls and cook 25–30 minutes, or until the stuffed lasagne is heated through.

Semolina gnocchi

Semolina gnocchi

Serves 4

2½ cups milk
1 cup coarse semolina
1 teaspoon salt
shake of pepper
¼ cup (½ stick) butter
¾ cup grated Parmesan cheese
¼ teaspoon ground nutmeg
1 large egg, beaten
extra butter

Pour the milk into a saucepan. Add the semolina, salt, pepper and butter. Stir constantly over low heat until the mixture comes to a boil and thickens. Continue to simmer until the mixture is very thick, for 5–7 minutes. Stir frequently to prevent the mixture sticking.

Remove from the heat and beat in ½ cup cheese and the nutmeg and egg. Beat until well mixed, then turn the mixture onto a flat dish, spreading it ¼-inch thick. Leave in a cool place for several hours, or until firm. Cut the gnocchi into ½-inch squares or circles with a knife or cookie cutter dipped in cold water.

Preheat oven to 425°. Butter a shallow ovenproof dish and fill it with layers of gnocchi squares or circles, arranged in overlapping circles. Sprinkle with the rest of the cheese and dot with the extra butter. Reheat and brown in the top of the oven 15 minutes.

Neapolitan pizza

Neapolitan pizza

Serves 2

Basic pizza dough
¼ teaspoon sugar
⅝ cup warm water
1 teaspoon dried yeast
2 cups all-purpose flour
1 teaspoon salt
1 tablespoon butter
For the filling
olive oil
6 medium tomatoes, peeled and sliced
1 garlic clove, chopped
12 anchovy fillets
¼ lb mozzarella cheese, thinly sliced
12 large black olives, pitted
oregano
pepper

Make the dough: Dissolve the sugar in the warm water and sprinkle the dried yeast on top. Leave the mixture in a warm place for 10–15 minutes, until it is frothy. Meanwhile, sift the flour and salt into a bowl and rub in the butter. Mix to a dough with the yeast liquid, adding a little extra flour if the dough is too sticky. Knead for about 10 minutes, until the dough is smooth and elastic, then put it in an oiled bowl. Cover with oiled paper and leave in a warm place to rise until the dough has doubled in size.

Preheat oven to 450°. Turn the dough onto a floured board, and knead slightly until it is smooth. Roll out into a circle ¼-inch thick and place it on an oiled cookie sheet. Brush the dough with olive oil and cover it with slices of tomato. Sprinkle with garlic, then top with anchovy fillets, cheese slices and olives. Sprinkle with oregano and pepper and bake near the top of the oven 25–30 minutes. Serve hot.

Variations: In place of the anchovies, ½ cup chopped cooked ham or 6–8 slices of salami. Omit the cheese and anchovies and use 1 cup sliced mushrooms (first fried in a little butter) and use sliced pimiento-stuffed green olives in place of black olives.

Fish

Above: Sole normande; Opposite above: Sole with savoury butter;
Opposite below: Crab with black beans

Sole Normande
Serves 4 to 6

2½ cups mussels
1¼ cups water
bouquet garni
salt and pepper
1 cup shrimp, thawed if frozen
a few oysters
1 onion, chopped
¾ cup white wine
8 fillets of sole, folded in half
6 tablespoons butter
½ cup all-purpose flour
½ cup milk
¾ cup heavy cream
1 cup sliced button mushrooms

Wash the mussels: Scrub them well and remove any
'beard' or weed attached to the shell. Discard any
mussels which do not close when sharply tapped,
because this means the mussel is dead. Put the
mussels in a pan with the water, bouquet garni and
seasoning. Heat until the mussels open, then lift them
out of the liquid. Shell the shrimp and shuck the
oysters. Put shrimp shells, the liquid from oyster
shells, the onion and wine in the mussel liquid.
Simmer for 15 minutes. Strain carefully and return
the liquid to the pan. Put the folded fillets of sole in
the pan and simmer until just tender. Lift the sole out
of the liquid and arrange on a hot flat dish or
individual serving dishes.

Melt 4 tablespoons of the cup butter in a saucepan,
stir in the flour and cook 2 minutes. Then blend in
the milk and the cream and a little of the strained fish
liquid. Bring slowly to the boiling point and cook
until thickened, stirring continually.

Cook the mushrooms in the remaining butter and
add to the sauce with the shellfish. Heat gently for 1–
2 minutes and spoon the sauce over the sole.

Sole with savory butter

Allow one whole sole, or flounder, per person and have them skinned on both sides. Place them in the preheated broiler pan, heavily brushed with melted butter. Brush the soles with more butter, sprinkle with salt and pepper and broil for 5–6 minutes. Turn the fish over, brush with more butter and broil for 5–6 minutes more. Serve immediately with lemon slices and Savory Butter pats. Garnish with parsley.

Crab with black beans
Serves 4

2 cans (about 7 oz each) crab meat
$\frac{1}{4}$ cup black beans
1 garlic clove, crushed
2 teaspoons dry sherry
2 teaspoons oil
pinch of ground ginger

Drain the crab and chop the meat finely and arrange it on the bottom of a greased heatproof dish.

Put the beans in boiling water, bring them back to a boil, then drain them and cool under cold running water. Mash them with a fork. Mix the beans with the garlic, sherry, oil and ginger. Beat the mixture well to make a smooth paste. Spread this mixture over the crab. Cover the dish and steam gently for 45 minutes, then serve in the dish.

Shrimp balls in sweet and sour sauce

Serves 4 to 6

Above: Shrimp balls in sweet and sour sauce
Below: Broiled trout

1 cup self-rising flour
salt
1 egg, beaten
$\frac{3}{4}$ cup water
1 lb jumbo shrimp, deveined, shelled and thawed if frozen
2 tablespoons cornstarch
$\frac{1}{2}$ teaspoon white pepper
pinch of monosodium glutamate
peanut oil, for deep frying
For the sauce
1 carrot, pared and cut into matchstick strips
1 green pepper, seeded, sliced and cut into matchstick strips
2 celery stalks, cut diagonally
little ground nut oil
3 tomatoes, peeled and chopped
$\frac{1}{4}$ cup vinegar
$\frac{1}{4}$ cup sugar
1 teaspoon very finely chopped fresh ginger
$\frac{1}{2}$ teaspoon salt
$1\frac{1}{2}$ teaspoons cornstarch
$\frac{3}{4}$ cup water

First cook the fish: Sift the flour and salt into a bowl. Make a well in the center and add the egg. Using a wooden spoon, mix the flour into the egg, add half the water and continue mixing, drawing in the flour. Beat thoroughly and stir in remaining water. Cut the shrimp into chunks about 1-inch across. Mix the cornstarch with salt, pepper and monosodium glutamate. Coat the shrimp in this mixture, then dip in the batter, shaking off any excess. Fry gently in deep, hot oil until crisp and golden brown. Remove from the oil, Drain well on paper towels and keep hot.

Drop the carrot, green pepper and celery into boiling water and simmer for 5 minutes, then drain. Just cover the base of a pan with ground nut oil, heat and put in the vegetables and remaining sauce ingredients. Add the water and bring to a boil, stirring. Add the shrimp balls and simmer for 2 minutes. Serve with boiled rice.

Broiled trout

Allow one trout per person. Have the trout cleaned and have the heads left on, if desired. Wash the fish and dry on paper towels. Place them in a well-buttered preheated broiler pan and brush with melted butter. Broil for 6–8 minutes, depending on thickness. Turn the fish over, brush with more butter and broil for 6–8 minutes more.

Serve immediately, garnished with lemon wedges and parsley. Accompany with extra melted butter.

Mussels marinière

Mussels marinière

Serves 4

Mussels marinière are fresh mussels steamed in white wine, and regularly appear on the menus of many excellent restaurants along the Mediterranean coast in the south of France. If French shallots are available from a speciality shop substitute them for the scallions to create a more authentic flavor. Mussels, like all other shellfish, must be cleaned with extreme care. Scrub them, remove the 'beards' and immediately throw away any mussels that are even slightly open. They can cause food poisoning. Also throw away any that slide when the two halves are pushed because sand may have gotten inside, and that will make the dish very unappetizing.

Serve the cooked mussels on the half shell and use the shell to scoop up the delicious wine-flavoured sauce.

| 4 quarts fresh mussels |
| 2 tablespoons butter |
| 4 small onions, finely chopped |
| 1 garlic clove, crushed |
| 4 parsley sprigs |
| 2 sprigs fresh thyme, or $\frac{1}{4}$ teaspoon dried thyme |
| 1 bay leaf |
| freshly ground black pepper |
| $1\frac{1}{4}$ cups dry white wine |
| 2 tablespoons butter |
| 1 tablespoon all-purpose flour |
| salt |
| chopped parsley |

Scrape and clean each mussel with a strong knife, removing every trace of seaweed, mud and beard. Wash very well and discard any mussels which are not firmly closed.

Melt butter in a large saucepan, add the onions and garlic and cook until soft but not colored. Add the herbs, pepper and wine and then the mussels. Cover with a tightly fitting lid and cook quickly, shaking the pan constantly, until the mussels open – about 5–6 minutes.

Lift the mussels out of the pan, using a slotted spoon, discard the empty half of each shell and keep the mussels hot in a covered serving dish.

Reduce the cooking liquid to about $1\frac{1}{4}$ cups. Remove the fresh thyme, parsley sprigs and bay leaf. Blend the butter with the flour and drop it into the simmering stock a teaspoon at a time, beating until the broth is smooth and thickened. Check the seasoning and add salt if needed. Pour the sauce over the mussels and scatter with plenty of chopped parsley.

55

Above: Fish in a jacket; Above centre: Mixed fried fish; Above left: Halibut with egg and lemon sauce

Fish in a jacket
Serves 4

1 package (17¼ oz) frozen puff pastry, thawed, or pastry made with 2 cups flour

4 large flounder fillets

salt and pepper

2 tablespoons butter

¼ cup all-purpose flour

½ cup milk

1 cup chopped mushrooms

To glaze

1 egg, beaten

1 tablespoon water

To garnish

lemon slices

parsley sprigs

Roll out the dough thinly and cut into four squares large enough to wrap around the folded fish fillets. Lay the fillets flat on a board and season lightly.

Melt the butter in a saucepan, add the flour and cook for 2 minutes, stirring. Blend in the milk and slowly bring to a boil; cook until the sauce thickens, stirring continually. Add the mushrooms to the sauce and season well.

Spread the sauce over half of each fillet, then fold the other half over. Lay each fish on a corner of a square of dough. Fold the dough over to form a triangle and seal the edges.

Preheat the oven to 475°. Place the triangles on a cookie sheet and brush the tops with the beaten egg mixed with the water. Bake just above the center of the oven 10 minutes, then lower the heat and cook for 20–25 minutes more, or until the pastry is golden brown and well risen. Garnish with lemon slices and parsley sprigs.

Mixed fried fish
Serves 4

¾ lb assorted white fish

¾ lb assorted shellfish

flour

hot fat or oil, for deep frying

For the batter

1 cup all-purpose flour

good pinch of salt

3 tablespoons olive oil

1 cup tepid water

1 egg white

To serve

lemon wedges

tartar sauce

First prepare the batter: Sift the flour and salt into a bowl. Add the oil and gradually add enough tepid water to make a smooth, creamy batter. Leave to stand in a cool place for 2 hours.

Prepare the fish and cut it into small pieces.

Just before frying, beat the egg white stiffly and fold it into the batter. Dip the pieces of fish in flour, then in the batter. Deep fry in hot fat or oil. Drain well on paper towels and serve with lemon wedges and tartar sauce.

Halibut with egg and lemon sauce

Serves 4

1 large onion, thinly sliced
1 carrot, pared and sliced
1 halibut steak, about 1 lb
$\frac{3}{4}$ cup water
salt and pepper
juice and peeled rind of $\frac{1}{4}$ lemon
For the sauce
2 teaspoons cornstarch
1 lemon
1 egg, beaten
To garnish
$\frac{1}{2}$ cucumber, sliced
1 lemon, sliced
parsley sprig

Put the onion and carrot in a skillet and place the halibut on top. Add the water, seasoning and lemon juice and rind. Cover the skillet, bring to a boil, then cook gently for about 15 minutes. When the fish is opaque, it is cooked. Carefully lift out the fish and place it on a heated serving dish. Strain the liquid in the pan for use in the sauce.

Make the sauce: Blend the cornstarch with the strained lemon juice. Bring the fish liquid to a boil and pour it over the cornstarch mixture. Return the mixture to the pan and cook for 1 minute. Allow the mixture to cool a little, then pour it into a bowl over the beaten egg. Mix and pour the sauce over the fish.

Arrange the cucumber and lemon slices around the fish and garnish with the parsley sprig.

Normandy herrings

Serves 4

4 large herrings
salt and pepper
¼ cup all-purpose flour
3 dessert apples
½ cup (1 stick) butter
1 large onion, finely chopped
1 tablespoon lemon juice
parsley sprigs, to garnish

Coat the fish in flour seasoned with salt and pepper. Pare, core and chop two of the apples. Heat ¼ cup of the butter in a large skillet. Cook the chopped apples with the onion until the apples are soft and the onion is transparent. Put the mixture in a hot serving dish, sprinkle with the lemon juice and keep warm. Core and slice the remaining apple and cook the slices in the pan. Lift out and set aside.

Heat the remaining butter in the skillet and cook the fish on each side until tender. Place the fish on top of the apple and onion mixture. Garnish with the apple slices and parsley sprigs.

Left: Normandy herrings
Below left: Tuna Provençale

Tuna Provençale

Serves 4

2 cans (7 oz each) tuna
juice of ½ lemon
salt and freshly ground black pepper
4 anchovy fillets
1¼ tablespoons olive oil
1 onion, chopped
4 tomatoes, peeled, seeded and chopped
1 garlic clove, crushed
bouquet garni
½ cup white wine
chopped parsley, to garnish

Remove the tuna from the cans very carefully so that they stay in shape and place side-by-side in an ovenproof serving dish. Sprinkle with lemon juice and season lightly with salt and pepper. Arrange anchovy fillets on top.

Preheat oven to 350°. Heat the olive oil in a small saucepan, add the onion and cook until softened. Add tomatoes, garlic, bouquet garni and wine. Bring to a boil and boil rapidly, uncovered, until reduced and thickened. Pour the sauce over the tuna, cover and bake 10–15 minutes. Remove the bouquet garni and serve sprinkled with chopped parsley.

Chablis halibut
Serves 4

2 wineglasses Chablis or other dry
white wine

4 halibut steaks

salt and pepper

$\frac{1}{4}$ cup ($\frac{1}{2}$ stick) butter

To garnish

hot cooked or canned whole kernel corn

red pepper strips

parsley sprigs

Put the wine in a shallow dish and marinate the fish in it 1 hour, turning after 30 minutes. Lift fish out of the wine and season lightly. Melt the butter and brush the fish with it. Put the fish in a pre-heated broiler pan brushed with melted butter and broil for about 5 minutes. Turn the fish over, brush with melted butter and broil 5 minutes more, or until the fish is cooked. The fish is cooked when it is opaque all through and flakes easily with a fork. Serve garnished with the whole kernel corn, topped with red pepper, and sprinkled parsley.

Heat any wine left in the dish and pour it over the fish before serving.

Above: Chablis halibut
Below: Haddock and mushroom scallops

Haddock and mushroom scallops
Serves 6

6 potatoes, pared and boiled

little butter

little light cream or milk

$\frac{1}{2}$ lb fresh haddock

$\frac{1}{2}$ lb smoked haddock

$2\frac{1}{2}$ cups milk

3 tablespoons butter

$\frac{1}{4}$ cup all-purpose flour

1 cup small button mushrooms

salt and pepper

1 can (7 oz) whole kernel corn, drained

To garnish

4 tomatoes, cut into wedges

parsley sprigs

Mash the potatoes and mix with a little butter and enough cream or milk to give a soft consistency. Put the potato into a pastry bag with a $\frac{1}{2}$-inch rose tip and pipe a border around six scallop shells or heatproof dishes. Brown gently under a low broiler while preparing the fish. Put the fish in a saucepan with the milk and about one-third of the butter. Simmer steadily until tender, about 10 minutes. Lift the fish out of the milk and place it on a flat dish. Allow it to cool slightly, then skin and flake it.

Meanwhile, melt the remaining butter in a pan, stir in the flour and cook for 2 minutes. Strain the milk used for the fish into the pan. Bring gradually to a boil and cook until thickened, stirring constantly. Add the mushrooms, seasoning, flaked fish and some of the drained whole kernel corn. Put spoonfuls of the fish mixture inside the potato border of each shell or dish. Top with hot whole kernel corn. Garnish with wedges of tomato and parsley sprigs.

Salmon Walewska

Salmon Walewska
Serves 4

½ cup (1 stick) butter
4 salmon steaks
1½ tablespoons lemon juice
salt and pepper
3 egg yolks
1 small cooked lobster, removed from shell and diced
To garnish
cucumber slices
lemon wedges
lobster claws

Preheat the oven to 360°. Melt 2 tablespoons of the butter and brush it over the salmon. Sprinkle with ½ tablespoon lemon juice and season lightly. Put the salmon in an ovenproof dish, cover with foil, and bake 20–25 minutes in the center of the oven. The salmon should be just tender; do not overcook.

Put the egg yolks, a little seasoning and the remaining lemon juice in a bowl over a pan of hot water. Beat until the mixture is thick, then beat in the remaining butter in small pieces and the diced lobster. Keep warm but do not overheat or the sauce will curdle.

Place the salmon on a hot serving dish, spoon over the sauce and garnish with the cucumber, lemon and lobster claws.

Scallops with peppers
Serves 4

12 scallops
1 tablespoon oil or melted shortening
2 scallions, finely chopped
1 teaspoon salt
2 green or red peppers, seeded and cut into small strips
¼ cup water

Wash and trim the scallops. Cut each scallop into slices. Heat the oil or shortening and cook the scallops and scallions for about 3 minutes, stirring continually. Add the salt and mix well. Add the peppers with the water and bring to a boil, stirring. Then lower the heat and simmer for about 2 minutes. Serve immediately.

Breton-style scallops

Serves 4

12 scallops
½ cup (1 stick) butter, melted
¾ cup fine browned bread crumbs
½ garlic clove, well crushed
1 teaspoon finely chopped parsley
salt and freshly ground black pepper
To garnish
lemon slices
parsley sprigs

Trim and wash the scallops. Drain them and cut them into thick pieces. Grease four scallop shells or small ovenproof dishes with a little of the melted butter. Sprinkle with half the bread crumbs. Divide the sliced scallops equally between the four shells.

Preheat the oven to 325°. Mix the remaining bread crumbs with the garlic and parsley, and season. Cover the scallops with the bread crumb mixture and pour over the remaining melted butter. Bake, uncovered, 15–20 minutes. Serve in the shells or dishes in which they are cooked. Garnish with lemon slices and parsley sprigs.

Note: If the scallops are large, they may be cooked on skewers, as shown in the picture.

Above: Breton-style scallops
Below: Scallops with peppers

Meat & variety meats

Swiss veal

Swiss veal
Serves 8

Veal is one of the most popular meats in Switzerland, and this creamy veal and mushroom dish is often found on family dinner tables. It is quick to prepare and an economical way to use a very expensive meat. One of the reasons veal is not more frequently served in the United States is because of the cost. If veal is too expensive for this dish it can also be made with thinly-sliced pieces of chicken breasts.

3 lb boned leg of veal, cut into strips 2-inches long, $\frac{1}{4}$-inch thick

$\frac{3}{4}$ cup all-purpose flour

salt and pepper

$\frac{3}{4}$ cup (1$\frac{1}{2}$ sticks) butter

2 onions, finely chopped

1$\frac{1}{4}$ cups dry white wine

2 cups chopped mushrooms

1$\frac{1}{4}$ cups light cream

1 tablespoon chopped parsley

$\frac{1}{4}$ teaspoon paprika

Dip the pieces of veal in seasoned flour. Melt $\frac{1}{2}$ cup butter in a skillet and cook the veal and onions until lightly browned, stirring occasionally. Add the wine and cook over medium heat, stirring to a smooth consistency.

Cook the mushrooms in the remaining butter for 5 minutes. Then stir in the cream, parsley and paprika. Mix the veal mixture gently with the mushroom mixture and season with salt and pepper. Reheat gently without allowing it to boil. Serve with buttered noodles or sautéed potatoes and a tossed mixed green salad.

Veal mornay

Veal mornay
Serves 4

4 small slices ham
4 veal scallops
salt and pepper
little flour
1 egg, beaten
1 cup dry bread crumbs
$\frac{1}{4}$ cup ($\frac{1}{2}$ stick) butter
1 tablespoon olive oil
canned asparagus tips, to garnish
For the sauce
3 tablespoons butter
$\frac{1}{4}$ cup all-purpose flour
$\frac{3}{4}$ cup milk
$\frac{3}{4}$ cup white wine (or use $1\frac{1}{2}$ cups milk and omit wine)
1 teaspoon French-style mustard
salt and pepper
2 tablespoons heavy cream
1 cup grated Cheddar or Swiss cheese
For the garnish
boiled new potatoes
chopped parsley
lemon slices
few cooked peas or asparagus tips

Place the slices of ham so that they cover half of each piece of veal, then fold the veal to cover the ham. Dip the meat in seasoned flour, then in beaten egg and bread crumbs. Heat the butter and oil together in a large skillet and cook the veal quickly on each side until crisp and golden brown. Then lower the heat and continue cooking until tender. Lift the meat out of the pan and drain on paper towels.

Make the sauce: melt the butter in a saucepan, then stir in the flour and cook for 2 minutes. Gradually stir in the milk and bring to a boil. Continue cooking, stirring constantly, until the sauce thickens. Then lower the heat and add the wine, mustard and salt and pepper. Stir the cream and cheese into the sauce just before serving without allowing the sauce to boil.

Arrange the veal on a dish with a border of new potatoes tossed in parsley. Put a spoonful of sauce in the center of each piece of meat and top with a twist of lemon and a few asparagus tips. Serve the rest of the sauce separately in a sauce boat.

Veal rolls

Serves 4

2 bacon slices, chopped
1 tablespoon finely chopped fresh parsley
1 small garlic clove, crushed
$\frac{2}{3}$ cup fresh white bread crumbs
1 egg, beaten
8 veal scallops
2 tablespoons butter
1 tablespoon flour
$\frac{1}{2}$ cup chicken broth or water
$\frac{3}{4}$ cup dry white wine
salt and pepper
1 cup halved mushrooms
4 tomatoes, peeled and quartered
stuffed green olives, to garnish

Mix the bacon, parsley, garlic, bread crumbs and egg. Stuff the veal slices with this mixture, roll them up tightly and secure with fine string. Melt the butter in a skillet and cook the veal quickly until browned. Remove the veal from the skillet and place in an ovenproof casserole.

Preheat the oven to 325°. Add the flour to the skillet and cook for 1 minute. Then stir in the water or broth and wine, bring to a boil, add seasoning and pour over the veal. Cover and cook 1 hour. Add the mushrooms and quartered tomatoes 30 minutes before the end of the cooking time. Garnish with the stuffed olives before serving.

Above left: Veal rolls
Above centre: Veal scallopini Bolognese
Above right: Veal scallopini Milanese

Veal scallopini Bolognese
Serves 4

4 veal scallops
flour
salt and pepper
1 egg, beaten
1 cup dry white bread crumbs
$\frac{1}{4}$ cup ($\frac{1}{2}$ stick) butter
1 tablespoon olive oil
4 lean slices ham
grated Parmesan cheese
extra butter, thinly sliced

Coat the veal scallops lightly in seasoned flour, then dip them in beaten egg and coat with bread crumbs. Heat the butter and oil together in a skillet and cook the veal quickly on each side until golden brown. Return all four pieces of veal to the skillet and cover each with a slice of ham. Then sprinkle with cheese and top with the extra butter. Cover the skillet with a lid and cook for about 3 minutes, or until the cheese melts. Serve immediately

Veal scallopini Milanese
Serves 4

1 egg, beaten
salt and pepper
4 veal scallops
1 cup dry white bread crumbs
$\frac{1}{4}$ cup ($\frac{1}{2}$ stick) butter
1 tablespoon olive oil
To garnish
1 hard-boiled egg, chopped
1 lemon, thinly sliced
parsley sprigs

Season the egg with salt and pepper. Dip the veal scallops in the egg, then in the bread crumbs, pressing them on well with a spatula.

Melt the butter with the oil in a skillet. When it is foaming, cook the veal for 4–5 minutes on each side. Arrange the cooked veal pieces on a hot serving dish and garnish with the chopped hard-boiled egg, lemon slices and parsley sprigs.

Veal fricassée
Serves 4

1¼ lb veal breast, cut into 2-inch cubes
2 medium-sized onions, finely chopped
2½ cups chicken or veal broth
bouquet garni
salt and pepper
¼ cup (½ stick) butter
½ cup all-purpose flour
2 egg yolks
2 tablespoons lemon juice
¾ cup heavy cream
To garnish
4 bacon slices
6–8 slices of bread
1–2 lemons
parsley sprigs

Put the veal and the onions in a saucepan and add nearly all the broth. Bring the broth to a boil, remove any scum that comes to the surface and add the bouquet garni and seasoning. Cover the pan and simmer very slowly for 1½ hours. When the veal is tender, add the butter. Mix the flour with the remaining broth and add it to the veal liquid, stirring. Bring to a boil and cook steadily, stirring constantly, until the sauce thickens. Remove the bouquet garni.

Mix the egg yolks with the lemon juice and cream. Take the pan of veal off the heat and stir in the egg and cream mixture. Return the pan to the heat and simmer for 5 minutes, stirring constantly. Take care not to let the sauce boil or it may curdle.

Cut the bacon slices in half. Stretch them with the back of a knife and roll them. Put the bacon rolls on a skewer and broil. Toast the bread, remove the crusts and cut the toast into triangles.

Spoon the veal and sauce onto a hot serving dish and top with bacon rolls, triangles of lemon and parsley sprigs. Arrange the toast around the edge of the dish. Serve extra toast and lemon with the veal.

Turin-style veal scallopini
Serves 4

4 veal scallops
all-purpose flour, for dusting
salt and pepper
1 egg, beaten
½ cup dry white bread crumbs
½ cup grated Parmesan cheese
1 tablespoon butter
1 tablespoon olive oil
To garnish
4 tomato slices
4 anchovy fillets
lemon wedges

Coat the veal lightly in seasoned flour, then dip the pieces in the beaten egg. Mix the bread crumbs and grated cheese and coat the meat in this mixture. Heat the butter and oil together and cook the veal on both sides until golden brown and tender. Top each veal scallop with a tomato slice and an anchovy fillet. Garnish with lemon wedges.

Beef bourguignonne

Serves 10

4 lb round or sirloin steak, cut into 1-inch cubes
$\frac{1}{2}$ cup all-purpose flour
$\frac{1}{4}$ cup olive oil
$\frac{1}{2}$ cup (1 stick) butter
$\frac{1}{2}$ lb bacon or pork, diced
$\frac{1}{3}$ cup brandy
4 carrots, pared and chopped
2 leeks, sliced
2 medium-sized onions, chopped
2 garlic cloves, crushed
1 bouquet garni
4 teaspoons salt
freshly ground black pepper
$2\frac{1}{2}$ cups red wine
$2\frac{1}{2}$ cups beef broth
2 tablespoons cornstarch
2 cups small white onions
2 cups button mushrooms
extra oil and butter, for frying
juice of 1 large lemon
freshly chopped parsley, to garnish

Roll the beef cubes in the flour. Heat the oil and butter together in a large heavy-bottomed skillet and cook the bacon or pork until crisp, then transfer it to a large ovenproof casserole. Cook the beef in several batches until it is browned and sealed all over. Heat the brandy, set light to it and add it flaming to the meat. Then transfer the meat and juices to the casserole.

Preheat the oven to 325°. Cook the carrots, leeks, onions and garlic in the skillet until golden, then transfer them to the casserole. Add the bouquet garni, salt, pepper and wine to the casserole. Add the beef broth to the skillet and heat, stirring to loosen the sediment, then transfer to the casserole, stirring to blend all the ingredients. Cover and cook $1\frac{1}{2}$ to 2 hours. Remove the bouquet garni.

Mix the cornstarch with 2 tablespoons cold water to a smooth paste. Stir it into the casserole and bring back to a boiling point on top of the stove to thicken the sauce.

Cook the onions and mushrooms in extra oil and butter, add lemon juice and simmer until tender. Add to the casserole and serve with parsley sprinkled over the top.

Note: Beef bourguignonne is usually thickened with a flour and butter paste but blended cornstarch is more suitable for a large quantity. The dish may be cooked the night before it is needed. It should be cooled, covered and stored in the refrigerator, then reheated the next day for serving.

Carpetbag steaks

Carpetbag steaks
Serves 6

6 thick pieces of tenderloin or round steak
about 24 washed and cooked mussels, or shucked and sliced oysters
$\frac{1}{2}$ cup (1 stick) butter
1 tablespoon freshly chopped parsley
lemon juice
salt and pepper
To garnish
2 tomatoes, broiled and halved
fried mushrooms, stems removed
parsley sprigs

Split the steaks to make 'pockets'. Mix the mussels or oysters with half the butter, the chopped parsley, a squeeze of lemon juice and seasoning. Put the mixture in the 'pockets' of the steak and skewer firmly or sew with fine string or thread. Brush the steaks with the remaining butter and broil until tender. Remove the skewers or string or thread and serve garnished with broiled tomatoes, fried mushrooms and parsley sprigs.

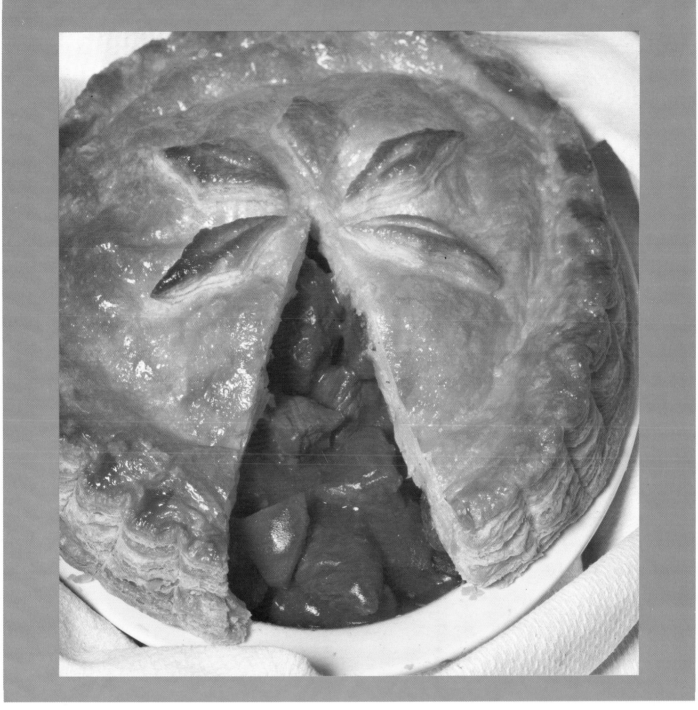

Steak and kidney pie

Steak and kidney pie

Serves 6

1 package (17¼ oz) frozen puff pastry, thawed
1 egg, to glaze
For the filling
1½ lb round steak, cut into 1-inch cubes
½ lb kidneys, skinned, cored and sliced
¼ cup all-purpose flour
salt and pepper
¼ cup dripping or shortening
2 cups beef broth

Roll the meat and kidneys in seasoned flour and cook gently in hot dripping or shortening. Gradually stir in the broth. Bring to a boil and cook until the broth has thickened, stirring constantly. Lower the heat, cover the pan tightly and cook gently until almost tender,

about 2–2½ hours. Make sure the liquid does not evaporate too much and add more if necessary.

Spoon the meat and a little gravy into a 6½–7½ cup deep pie plate and allow to cool.

Preheat oven to 450°. Roll out the dough and trim off a strip to go around the edge of the pie plate. Dampen the strip and cover the plate with dough. Trim off excess dough with a knife and make indentations at regular intervals around the edge. Make a slit in the center of the pie and decorate with leaves made from the trimmings. Brush with beaten egg mixed with a little water. Bake in the center of the oven 15 minutes, then lower the heat to 350° and cook for 30–35 minutes, or until the pastry is brown and firm.

Beef and prune stew
Serves 4

1¼ lb chuck steak, cut into 1-inch cubes
salt and pepper
¼ cup all-purpose flour
¼ cup shortening or dripping
about 18 prunes, soaked overnight in
2½ cups beef broth
1 tablespoon concentrated tomato paste
2 bay leaves
4 tomatoes, peeled

Roll the meat cubes in seasoned flour and cook in the hot shortening or dripping until they are browned all over. Strain the broth from the prunes and add it to the meat. Bring to a boil and cook until the broth has thickened. Add the tomato paste, about six finely-chopped pitted prunes and the bay leaves. Cover the pan and simmer for 1¾ hours. Add the rest of the prunes, whole, and cook for 15 minutes more. Then add the tomatoes and cook for another 15 minutes. Remove the bay leaves.

Upside-down steak pie
Serves 4

2 medium-sized onions, chopped
2–3 tomatoes, peeled and chopped
few mushrooms or mushroom stems, chopped
¼ cup shortening
1¼ cups beef broth
¾ lb lean ground beef
parsley sprigs, to garnish
For the topping
1½ cups self-rising flour
salt and pepper
¼ cup (½ stick) butter
½ cup finely grated Cheddar cheese
1 egg yolk
milk, to mix

Cook the vegetables in hot shortening until soft. Add the broth and the ground beef. Stir until smooth and thick and season well. Cook for 15 minutes, uncovered, stirring occasionally.

Preheat the oven to 350°. Meanwhile, prepare the topping: Sift the flour with seasoning. Rub in the butter and stir in the grated cheese. Bind with the egg yolk and add enough milk to make a soft rolling consistency. Form the dough into a circle about 7 inches in diameter. Put the meat mixture in a cake pan or ovenproof dish and top with the dough. Bake in the center of the oven about 50 minutes. Invert onto a hot dish and garnish with parsley. Serve with creamed carrots and sautéed potatoes.

Variation: This dish can be made with chopped chuck steak rather than ground beef. If using chuck, then simmer the mixture for about 1–1¼ hours, uncovered, replacing evaporated liquid as necessary.

Opposite left: Beef and prune stew
Centre: Upside-down steak pie
Above: Stuffed tenderloin beef

Stuffed beef tenderloin
Serves 4

3 medium-sized onions, sliced
beef dripping
4 anchovy fillets, chopped
2 tablespoons finely chopped bacon
pinch of pepper
pinch of dried thyme
pinch of finely chopped parsley
1 egg yolk
2 lb beef tenderloin
watercress sprigs, to garnish

Preheat oven to 325°. Cook the onions in about 1 tablespoon dripping until golden brown. Remove them from the skillet and place in a mixing bowl. Add the anchovy fillets, bacon, pepper, herbs and egg yolk to the onions and mix well. Cut the tenderloin in about six places, but not right through. Put some of the stuffing in each cavity and tie the tenderloin with string or secure with wooden toothpicks. Wrap in greased foil or place in a covered baking pan with a little dripping and cook 1½ hours or until tender. Cut into thick slices to serve and garnish with watercress sprigs.

Braised beef rolls
Serves 4

1 medium-sized onion, finely chopped
¾ lb kidneys, skinned, cored and finely chopped
1 tablespoon freshly chopped parsley
2 tablespoons margarine
salt and pepper
4 slices round steak or beef, halved
2 medium-sized onions, sliced
6 carrots, pared and sliced
¼ cup shortening
¼ cup all-purpose flour
1¼ cups beef broth
freshly chopped parsley, to garnish

Mix together the chopped onion, kidneys, chopped parsley, margarine and seasoning. Divide the mixture between the pieces of meat and roll up firmly. Secure with wooden toothpicks or string. Put the sliced onions and carrots in an ovenproof casserole.

Preheat the oven to 325°. Heat the shortening in a skillet. Coat the beef rolls in seasoned flour and cook them quickly in the shortening, until browned all over. Place the beef rolls on top of the vegetables in the casserole. Blend the broth with the juices in the skillet and pour it around the meat. Cover the casserole and cook in the coolest part of the oven about 1½ hours, or until the meat is tender. Sprinkle with chopped parsley before serving.

Beef and vegetable stew
Serves 4

1¾ lb chuck steak, cut into 1½-inch cubes
¼ cup all-purpose flour
salt and pepper
¼ cup shortening
8 baby white onions
2½ cups beef broth
8 small carrots, scraped
2–3 celery stalks
1 cup button mushrooms
bouquet garni
freshly chopped parsley, to garnish

Roll the meat in seasoned flour. Melt the shortening in a large saucepan and quickly cook meat and onions, turning the meat until it is browned all over. Stir in the broth gradually. Bring the liquid to a boil and stir well until it has thickened slightly. Add the remaining vegetables, leaving the carrots and mushrooms whole, and the bouquet garni. Season to taste and cover with a tight-fitting lid. Simmer 2¼–2½ hours, or until the meat is tender.

Remove the bouquet garni and serve in a hot dish. Garnish with chopped parsley.

Beef curry
Serves 4

1 tablespoon ground coriander
1 teaspoon ground turmeric
½ teaspoon cumin
¼ teaspoon chili powder
pinch of ground cinnamon
¼ teaspoon ground cloves
3 tablespoons vinegar
2 tablespoons vegetable oil
1 medium-sized onion, chopped
1 garlic clove, crushed
1 lb round steak or beef, cut into 1-inch cubes
1 teaspoon salt
¾ cup beef broth
1 bay leaf
freshly cut orange wedges, to garnish
boiled rice, to serve
mango chutney, to serve

Mix and pound the spices with the vinegar to form a paste. Heat the oil in a heavy-bottomed skillet and cook the onion and garlic gently for 5 minutes. Add the curry paste and cook for 2–3 minutes, stirring constantly. Add the beef and cook gently, stirring occasionally, until it browns. Add salt, broth and bay leaf, cover and simmer for 1 hour. Remove the bay leaf, taste the curry and adjust the seasoning if necessary. Garnish with orange wedges. Serve with boiled rice and chutney.

Opposite: Braised beef rolls
Below: Beef and vegetable stew
Below right: Beef curry

Pepperpot beef
Serves 6

¼ cup all-purpose flour
1 teaspoon salt
pinch of pepper
½ teaspoon ground ginger
2 lb round steak, cut into 1-inch cubes
¼ cup shortening or dripping
1 small red pepper, seeded, sliced and diced
1 can (about 1 lb) red kidney beans, drained

For the sauce

1 teaspoon chili sauce
1 can (about 8 oz) tomatoes, with the juices
1 cup sliced mushrooms
1 tablespoon Worcestershire sauce
2 tablespoons wine vinegar
2 garlic cloves, crushed
1 bay leaf

Mix the flour, seasoning and ginger and coat the beef cubes with it. Melt the shortening or dripping in a large skillet and quickly cook the beef until it is browned, turning once. Drain on paper towels, then transfer it to an ovenproof casserole.

Preheat the oven to 325°. Combine all the ingredients for the sauce and pour over the meat.

Cover and cook about 2 hours or until the meat is tender. Add the red pepper and kidney beans 30 minutes before the end of the cooking time.

Hamburgers
Serves 4

1 lb lean ground beef
1 egg or egg yolk
salt and pepper
pinch of dried mixed herbs
flour
shortening, for frying
4 hamburger buns
favorite accompaniments

Mix the meat, egg or egg yolk, seasoning and herbs. Form the mixture into four flat patties with floured hands. Cook in a little hot shortening for 3–4 minutes on each side. Serve in the buns with your favorite accompaniments.

Hamburgers may be served with catsup, onion rings, horseradish sauce, chutney and any other relishes of your choice.

Below left: Pepperpot beef
Below: Hamburgers
Above: Killarney hot-pot

Killarney hot-pot
Serves 4 to 6

6 potatoes, pared and sliced

salt and pepper

4 medium-sized onions, sliced

2–3 large carrots, pared and sliced

½ lb ham, diced

1 lb lean brisket, cut into 1-inch cubes

¼ teaspoon dried sage

¾ cup dark beer

2 tablespoons butter

Put one-third of the potatoes in an ovenproof casserole and season well. Then put in half the onions, carrots and meat, seasoning each layer, and sprinkling a little sage over the meat. Put in another layer of potatoes, keeping some for the top, and the remaining onions, carrots and meat. Pour over the beer, then arrange the remaining potatoes on top and dot with butter.

Preheat the oven to 325°. Cook for 2 hours in the center of the oven. Leave the casserole uncovered for the first 15 minutes of cooking so that the butter melts and coats the potatoes. Then remove the lid 20 minutes before the end of cooking, to brown the potatoes.

Pork and bamboo shoots

Pork and bamboo shoots
Serves 6 to 8

3 tablespoons soy sauce
1 tablespoon dry sherry
1 teaspoon light brown sugar
1 teaspoon ground ginger
2 lb pack tenderloin, cut into 1-inch cubes
5 cups water
2 cups canned bamboo shoots, drained and shredded

Mix together the soy sauce, sherry, sugar and ginger in a bowl. Add the pork cubes, toss them well and leave to marinate for 10 minutes.

Put the pork and marinade into a large saucepan, add the water and bring gently to a boil, then cover and simmer for 1 hour. Add the bamboo shoots and simmer for 10 minutes. Serve immediately.

Note: The liquid may be thickened slightly with 1 tablespoon cornstarch mixed to a smooth paste with a little cold water.

Ham and sweet peppers
Serves 4

3 red peppers, seeded and shredded
1 tablespoon cornstarch
2 tablespoons soy sauce
1 tablespoon dry sherry
1 teaspoon sugar
2 tablespoons broth or water
$\frac{3}{4}$ lb cubed ham
2 tablespoons vegetable oil

Cover the shredded peppers with boiling water and leave for 1 minute to blanch, then drain. Mix the cornstarch, soy sauce, sherry, sugar and broth or water. Pour the mixture over the ham and mix well so that the meat is completely coated. Heat the oil in a skillet or wok and cook the peppers 2 minutes over fierce heat, stirring constantly. Remove the peppers from the skillet or wok. Put the ham into the skillet with the liquid, and cook for 1 minute, stirring constantly, over medium heat. Add the peppers, cook for another minute, then serve.

Above: Ham and sweet peppers; Below: Normandy-style pork

Normandy-style pork
Serves 6

6 thick pork chops
shortening for cooking
2 medium-sized onions, chopped
1¼ cups dry white wine
1 tablespoon Calvados (optional)
pinch of sage
2–3 dessert apples, pared, cored and chopped
salt and pepper
little olive oil

Cook the chops in hot shortening in a large skillet for
5–8 minutes, or until lightly browned. Lift them out
of the pan. Cook the onions in the pan until tender
but not brown. Add the wine, Calvados, sage, apples
and seasoning. Preheat the oven to 350°. Put the
mixture in a large ovenproof casserole and put the
chops on top. Keep the skin uppermost so that it
crisps and brush with oil. Do not cover. Cook for 40–
45 minutes in the center of the oven.

Ham with pineapple and corn sauce

Serves 4

4 ham slices
$\frac{1}{4}$ cup ($\frac{1}{2}$ stick) butter, melted
4 rings of canned pineapple, drained with juice reserved
watercress, to garnish
For the sauce
2 tablespoons butter
$\frac{1}{4}$ cup all-purpose flour
$1\frac{1}{4}$ cups milk
1 medium-sized onion, finely chopped
salt and pepper
4 tablespoons cooked or canned whole kernel corn
2 teaspoons chopped parsley
2 tablespoons juice from pineapple
1 bunch watercress, to garnish

Cut the edges of the ham to prevent it curling. Brush the ham with melted butter and broil for several minutes, then turn it, brush with more butter and broil for several minutes on the other side. When the ham is almost cooked, brush the pineapple rings with melted butter and put them on the broiler pan to heat.

While the ham is cooking, make the sauce: melt the butter in a saucepan, add the flour and cook for 2 minutes, stirring constantly. Gradually blend in the milk, still stirring, and add the onion. Bring the sauce to a boil and cook until it has thickened, stirring constantly. Season the sauce and add the whole kernel corn and parsley. When ready to serve, beat in the pineapple juice.

Arrange the ham on a hot serving dish and put the pineapple slices on top. Garnish with watercress and serve the sauce separately.

Sweet and sour pork with lychees

Serves 4 to 6

3 tablespoons soy sauce
1 tablespoon dry sherry
1 teaspoon very finely chopped fresh ginger
pinch of monosodium glutamate
1 lb picnic roast pork, cut into 1-inch cubes
$\frac{1}{4}$ cup all-purpose flour
$\frac{1}{4}$ cup cornstarch
pinch of salt
2 eggs, beaten
vegetable oil, for deep frying
$\frac{1}{2}$ red pepper, seeded and cut into 1-inch squares
$\frac{1}{2}$ green pepper, seeded and cut into 1-inch squares
2 apples, pared, cored and quartered
1 tablespoon light brown sugar
$\frac{3}{4}$ cup syrup from canned lychees
2 tablespoons vinegar
4 scallions, finely chopped
1 can (about $\frac{3}{4}$ lb) lychees, drained
extra 1 tablespoon cornstarch
extra 1 tablespoon soy sauce
salt

Mix together in a bowl the soy sauce, sherry, ginger and monosodium glutamate. Add the pork cubes, stir to coat and marinate for 1–2 hours.

Sift the flour, cornstarch and salt into a bowl. Add the eggs gradually, beating well to make a smooth batter. Coat the pork cubes in the batter, shaking off any excess. Deep fry gently in hot oil until golden brown. Remove from the oil, drain them on paper towels and keep hot.

Mix all the remaining ingredients in a small saucepan. Bring to the boil, stirring constantly, and simmer for 2–3 minutes. Put the pork on a heated serving dish and pour over the sauce. Serve immediately.

Ham with pineapple and corn sauce

Stuffed ham rolls

Serves 4

Above: Sweet and sour pork with lychees
Below: Stuffed ham rolls

2 celery stalks, chopped	
2 apples, pared, cored and chopped	
$\frac{1}{2}$ cup finely chopped walnuts	
1 tablespoon chopped chives	
1 tablespoon lemon juice	
$\frac{3}{4}$ cup thick mayonnaise	
salt and pepper	
8 ham slices	
$\frac{1}{4}$ lb chicken liver pâté	
To garnish	
fresh parsley sprigs	
1 lemon, thinly sliced	

Mix together the celery, apples, walnuts, chives and lemon juice. Add the mayonnaise, then taste and adjust seasoning. Spread each slice of ham with pâté. Divide the mayonnaise mixture between the slices and roll them up. Garnish with parsley sprigs and lemon slices.

Above: Loin of lamb with navy beans; Above right: Roast lamb with apricot-nut stuffing

Loin of lamb with navy beans
Serves 4

1⅓ cups navy beans, soaked overnight and drained
salt
1 carrot, pared and chopped
1 onion, peeled and sliced
bouquet garni
2 lb boneless loin of lamb
1 garlic clove, sliced
1¼ cups beef broth
2 large tomatoes, peeled, seeded and chopped
freshly chopped parsley, to garnish

Place the beans in a large saucepan with cold water to cover. Add the carrot, onion and bouquet garni. Bring to a boil and simmer for 2 hours, or until tender.

Preheat the oven to 375°. Meanwhile, wipe the lamb and rub all over with salt. Place slices of garlic in various places under the skin of the lamb. Roll the meat and tie with fine string. Place the lamb in a lightly greased baking pan with the broth, cover with waxed paper and roast 50 minutes. After 20 minutes remove the paper and baste with the broth in the pan, then replace the paper. Baste two or three more times during cooking and remove the paper for the last 10 minutes, to brown.

Place the meat on a heated serving dish and keep hot. Drain the cooked beans. Reserve the onion and carrot pieces. Mix the beans with the tomatoes, carrot and onion and a little of the meat broth to moisten. Spoon the beans around the meat and garnish with the chopped parsley.

Roast lamb with apricot-nut stuffing
Serves 6

boneless shoulder of lamb
2–4 tablespoons shortening
For the stuffing
1 can (about ½ lb) apricots, drained and chopped, with some juice reserved
1 cup fresh bread crumbs
½ cup finely chopped walnuts
¼ cup (½ stick) butter, softened
juice of 1 orange and 1 lemon
salt and pepper
1 egg, beaten
mint jelly, to serve

Combine all the ingredients for the stuffing and moisten with a little juice from the apricots, if necessary. Spread the stuffing over the meat, roll up and tie with fine string. Weigh the meat to calculate cooking time.

Preheat the oven to 425°. Put the meat in a roasting pan and spread shortening over it. Cook 15 minutes, then lower the heat to 375°. Allow 20 minutes per lb and 20 minutes over (slightly less if you like the meat rare). For slow roasting, preheat oven at 350° and cook for 35 minutes per 1 lb and 35 minutes over. Serve with thin gravy and mint jelly.

Simple cassoulet

Serves 4
Like many other favorite Frensh dishes, cassoulets were first cooked in farmhouse kitchens by farmers' wives who did not have any time for the formalities or expense of Parisian cuisine. It is a simple dish, popular throughout the world because of its rich flavors. A traditional cassoulet contains salt belly of pork, which is often difficult to get in this country, so instead this simple version uses reserved bacon fat to add extra flavor. It is also essential to use fresh, not frozen, vegetables.

2 tablespoons reserved bacon fat
1½ lb stewing lamb, cut into 1-inch cubes
2 onions, peeled and thinly sliced
2 cups water or broth
½ cup tomato paste
1 cup lima or navy beans, soaked overnight and drained
2 carrots, pared and sliced
1 parsnip, pared and sliced
1 celery stalk, sliced
pinch of dried thyme
1 bay leaf
freshly ground black pepper
salt
parsley sprig, to garnish

Melt the bacon fat in a large, heavy-bottomed saucepan and cook the lamb and onions until the lamb is lightly browned and the onions transparent. Pour in a little water or broth and stir in the tomato paste. Add the rest of the water or broth, the beans, carrots, parsnip, celery, herbs and pepper and stir well. Bring gently to a boil, then cover and simmer until the meat is very tender, about 2 hours. Add salt and simmer gently for a final 30 minutes, 30–40 uncovered.

81

Kabobs

Serves 4

1 lb tenderloin pork, cut into 1-inch cubes
good pinch of ground allspice
salt and pepper
4 medium-sized onions, quartered
8 tomatoes, halved or quartered
2 green peppers, seeded and cut into 1-inch squares
vegetable oil
For serving
1¼ cups long grain rice
2 tablespoons vegetable oil
2½ cups broth

Toss the rice in hot oil, then add the broth and cook until the broth is absorbed and the rice is tender. While the rice is cooking, prepare the kabobs: roll the pork in the allspice and seasoning. Arrange the meat, onions, tomatoes and peppers alternately on lightly-oiled skewers. Brush them with vegetable oil and broil, turning, while they cook so that the meat browns evenly all over basting with more oil as necessary.

Place the rice on a hot serving dish and arrange the kabobs on top.

Crown roast of lamb

Have a crown roast prepared by the butcher or meat department of a supermarket.

Stuff and cook as for Roast lamb with apricot-nut stuffing, using the same stuffing or a package stuffing. If preferred, cook without stuffing and fill the center with cooked vegetables, for serving. Put foil on the ends of the bones to prevent them from scorching while cooking.

Crown roast of lamb is equally impressive to serve for a family meal or as the main course of a special dinner party.

Above left: Kabobs
Above right: Crown roast of lamb
Opposite: French-style tripe (top),
Oxtail hotch-potch with mustard
dumplings (left), Fricassée of
sweetbreads (right), Kidneys
bordelaise (bottom) (recipes overleaf)

French style tripe

Serves 6

2 lb tripe

2 tablespoons vegetable oil

3 medium-sized onions, sliced

3 carrots, pared and sliced

1 cup sliced mushrooms

1 garlic clove, crushed

1 tablespoon all-purpose flour

1¼ cups chicken broth

salt and pepper

¼ cup light cream

2 tablespoons brandy or dry sherry

Cut the tripe into neat pieces and wash it in cold water. Put it in a saucepan, cover with cold water and bring to a boil to blanch it. Strain off the liquid and discard.

Heat the oil in a saucepan and cook the vegetables and garlic for a few minutes. Stir in the flour and cook for 2 minutes. Then stir in the broth and bring it to a boil. Add the tripe and season. Lower the heat, cover the pan tightly and simmer for 40 minutes, or until tender. Mix the cream with the brandy or sherry and add it to the tripe. Cook without boiling for 5 minutes.

Oxtail hotch-potch
with mustard dumplings

Serves 4 to 6

1 good-sized oxtail, cut up

3 medium-sized onions, sliced

3 large carrots, pared and sliced

5 cups water or beef broth

grated rind of 1 lemon

bouquet garni

salt and pepper

¼ cup cornstarch

For the dumplings

1 cup self-rising flour

1 teaspoon mustard powder

salt and pepper

¼ cup chopped suet or beef dripping frozen and put through a meat grinder

water, to mix

Put the oxtail in a large, heavy-bottomed saucepan and cook it in its own fat until golden brown. Then lift it out of the saucepan and put in the onions and half the carrots. Cook them in the fat in the pan for about 5 minutes. Strain off any surplus fat, then put the oxtail back in the pan and add the water or broth, lemon rind, bouquet garni and seasoning. Simmer for 1½ hours. Then add the remaining carrot slices and simmer for 1 hour. Let the meat become quite cold then remove the surplus fat. Reheat and add the cornstarch blended with a little cold water, stirring well until the sauce thickens.

While the oxtail is cooking, make the dumplings: sift the flour with the mustard and seasoning. Add the suet and enough water to make a soft dough. Roll into eight balls with floured hands. Bring the oxtail liquid to a boil, drop in the dumplings, then cook steadily for 20 minutes.

Fricassée of sweetbreads

Serves 5 to 6

1½ lb sweetbreads

1¼ cups chicken broth

1 medium-sized onion

bouquet garni

thinly peeled rind of 1 lemon

little lemon juice

salt and pepper

2 tablespoons butter

2 tablespoons all-purpose flour

1¼ cups milk

1 tablespoon chopped parsley

2 tablespoons light cream

To garnish

3–4 slices of bread

¼ cup shortening or butter

Wash the sweetbreads in cold water, then put in a saucepan and cover with cold water. Bring the water to a boil to blanch, then drain and discard the liquid. Put the sweetbreads in a saucepan with the broth, whole peeled onion, bouquet garni, lemon rind and a little lemon juice. Season well and simmer gently for 30–35 minutes, or until the sweetbreads are tender. Strain off the broth and reserve it. Allow the sweetbreads to cool, then remove any pieces of skin.

Melt the butter in a saucepan, stir in the flour and cook for 2 minutes. Gradually blend in the milk, stirring constantly. Bring to a boil, then lower the heat and cook until thickened, stirring constantly. Stir about ¾ cup of the reserved cooking liquid into the sauce. Put in the sweetbreads and heat thoroughly. Add the chopped parsley, extra seasoning, if necessary, and the cream.

While the sweetbreads are cooking, remove the crusts from the bread and cut the slices into triangles. Cook them in hot shortening or butter until golden brown. Place the sweetbreads in a hot serving dish and arrange the fried bread around the edge.

Creamed kidneys

Kidneys bordelaise
Serves 5 to 6

about 20 lambs' kidneys, skinned, cored and halved
$\frac{1}{2}$ cup all-purpose flour
salt and pepper
pinch of ground nutmeg
$\frac{1}{4}$ cup ($\frac{1}{2}$ stick) butter
2 medium-sized onions, sliced
2 bacon slices, cut into narrow strips
1 tablespoon chopped parsley
$1\frac{1}{4}$ cups beef broth
$\frac{3}{4}$ cup red wine
3 cups creamed potatoes, to serve
parsley sprigs, to garnish

Roll the kidneys in the flour mixed with seasoning and nutmeg. Melt the butter in a large casserole and cook the onions and bacon gently for a few minutes. Add the kidneys and cook gently for 5 minutes, stirring well. Add the chopped parsley, then gradually blend in the broth and wine. Bring the sauce to a boil, then lower the heat and cook until thickened, stirring constantly. Cover the pan and simmer for about 15 minutes.

Meanwhile, pipe the creamed potatoes around the edge of a serving dish and brown under the broiler. Spoon the kidney mixture into the center of the potato ring and garnish with parsley sprigs.

Creamed kidneys
Serves 3 to 4

1 green pepper, seeded and cut into strips
1 red pepper, seeded and cut into strips
salt and pepper
8 lambs' kidneys, skinned, cored and sliced
$\frac{1}{4}$ cup all-purpose flour
$\frac{1}{4}$ cup ($\frac{1}{2}$ stick) butter
3 tablespoons dry sherry
$\frac{3}{4}$ cup light cream
1 cup long grain rice

Blanch the strips of pepper by cooking them in boiling seasoned water for 3–4 minutes, then drain. Roll the kidneys in seasoned flour. Melt the butter in a large saucepan and cook the peppers for a few minutes, then lift them out and keep hot. Cook the kidneys in the pan for 8–10 minutes, or until tender. Turn the meat several times while cooking. Mix the sherry and cream in a bowl. Remove the pan from the heat, add the sherry and cream mixture and stir well. Return to low heat for 2–3 minutes and add the peppers to heat through.

While the kidneys and peppers are being prepared, cook the rice in boiling salted water. Drain and arrange in a ring in a hot dish. Spoon the kidneys and peppers in the center of the ring.

Above: Sicilian-style liver; Above right: Kidney kabobs with orange sauce

Sicilian-style liver
Serves 4 to 6

$1\frac{1}{4}$ lb calf liver, cut into strips
$\frac{1}{4}$ cup all-purpose flour
salt and pepper
$\frac{1}{4}$ cup shortening or fat
3 medium-sized onions, sliced
1 garlic clove, crushed
$1\frac{1}{4}$ cups broth
$1\frac{1}{4}$ cups red wine
1 tablespoon red currant jelly
$\frac{1}{2}$ teaspoon grated lemon rind
3 tablespoons stuffed olives

Coat the liver with seasoned flour. Melt the shortening or fat in a pan and quickly brown the liver in it. Then lift out the liver and cook the onion rings and garlic for a few minutes. Gradually blend in the broth and wine, then bring to a boil and cook until slightly thickened. Add the red currant jelly and lemon rind. Replace the liver, cover the pan and simmer very slowly for about 2 hours. Add the olives just before serving. Serve with creamed potatoes, boiled rice or noodles.

Variation: Sicilian-style beef can be made in a similar way – use good-quality chuck steak cut into 1-inch cubes. Cook for the same amount of time.

Kidney kabobs with orange sauce
Serves 4

8–12 lambs' kidneys, skinned, cored and halved
salt and pepper
pinch of dried mixed herbs
12 button mushrooms
12 baby white onions
4 bacon slices, halved and rolled up
$\frac{1}{4}$ cup ($\frac{1}{2}$ stick) butter, melted
boiled rice, to serve
For the sauce
thinly peeled rind and juice of 2 oranges
$1\frac{1}{4}$ cups beef broth
$\frac{1}{4}$ cup cornstarch
2 tablespoons butter
salt and pepper
$\frac{1}{2}$ teaspoon sugar

Roll the kidneys in seasoning and herbs. Put them alternately on skewers with the mushrooms, onions and rolled bacon. Brush with the melted butter and cook under a hot broiler for about 8 minutes. Turn several times during cooking so all the ingredients cook evenly.

Make the sauce: Simmer the rind in half the broth for about 5 minutes. Then strain the broth and return it to the saucepan. Mix the cornstarch with the rest of the broth and add it to the pan with the orange juice, butter, seasoning and sugar. Stir well and bring the sauce to a boil. Then lower heat and cook gently until the sauce is smooth and thickened, stirring constantly. Segments of orange may be added, if wished. Serve the kabobs on a bed of boiled rice, with the sauce.

Kidneys with scallions and cauliflower

Kidneys with scallions and cauliflower

Serves 3 to 4

4 lambs' kidneys, skinned, cored and sliced
2 tablespoons dry sherry
1 small cauliflower, in flowerets
2 tablespoons vegetable oil
4 scallions, cut into 1-inch pieces
1 tablespoon cornstarch
1 tablespoon soy sauce
1 teaspoon brown sugar
1 teaspoon salt

Soak the kidneys in the sherry. Cook the cauliflower in boiling salted water for 3 minutes, then drain. Melt the oil in a skillet or wok. Drain the kidneys, reserving the sherry, then cook the kidneys and cauliflower with the scallions for 2 minutes. Mix the cornstarch to a smooth paste with the soy sauce, 2 tablespoons water, sugar, reserved sherry and salt. Add to the skillet and cook gently for 3 minutes, stirring constantly. Serve with boiled rice.

Stir-fried liver and scallions

Serves 4

1 lb calf liver, cut in small slices	
1 tablespoon cornstarch	
2 tablespoons dry sherry	
2 tablespoons soy sauce	
2 tablespoons vegetable oil	
2 scallions, finely chopped	
2 leeks, thoroughly washed and thickly sliced	
1 teaspoon brown sugar	
pinch of salt	

Cover the liver with boiling water and leave for 1 minute, then drain. Mix the cornstarch, sherry and soy sauce to a smooth paste, add to the liver and mix well. Heat the oil in a skillet or wok and cook the liver for 1 minute over fierce heat, stirring constantly. Add the scallions, leeks, sugar, salt and any remaining cornstarch mixture. Heat quickly, stirring, for 1 minute. Serve with boiled rice.

Lemon-garlic kidneys
Serves 4

12 lambs' kidneys, skinned, cored and sliced
salt and pepper
1 garlic clove, finely chopped
2 tablespoons olive oil
freshly squeezed juice of 1 lemon
boiled rice, to serve
lemon wedges, to garnish

Season the kidneys and cook them with the garlic in hot oil for 3–4 minutes, turning constantly. Squeeze the lemon juice over the kidneys and remove from the heat. Serve on a bed of boiled rice and garnish with lemon wedges.

Braised liver with mushrooms and rice
Serves 3

2 tablespoons butter
$\frac{1}{2}$ small onion, finely grated
1 tablespoon all-purpose flour
$\frac{1}{4}$ teaspoon salt
pinch of pepper
$\frac{1}{2}$ lb lamb's liver, chopped
2 cups sliced mushrooms
$\frac{1}{2}$ cup broth
1 cup long-grain rice
To garnish
parsley sprigs
paprika

Preheat the oven to 325°. Melt the butter in a skillet and cook the onion gently until soft. Mix together the flour, salt and pepper and coat the pieces of liver. Add the liver to the skillet and cook gently with the onion. Add the mushrooms and cook for a few minutes. Then add the broth and bring to a boil. Place the contents of the skillet in an ovenproof casserole and cover tightly. Cook 45 minutes.

Meanwhile, cook the rice in plenty of boiling salted water until tender but not mushy. Drain the rice and rinse in hot water, then press it into a lightly-greased ring mold. Press the rice down tightly, then turn it into a hot dish. Put the cooked liver mixture in the center of the rice ring. Garnish with parsley and sprinkle over paprika.

Opposite: Stir-fried liver and scallions
Above right: Lemon-garlic kidneys
Right: Braised liver with mushrooms and rice

Poultry & game dishes

Chicken with white wine and mushrooms

Chicken with white wine and mushrooms
Serves 4

1 boiler/fryer, about 3 lb
$\frac{1}{4}$ cup ($\frac{1}{2}$ stick) butter
12 baby white onions
8 slices bacon, diced
2 tablespoons all-purpose flour
1 cup button mushrooms
$\frac{1}{2}$ cup white wine
$\frac{3}{4}$ cup chicken broth
bouquet garni
salt and freshly ground black pepper

Cut the chicken into four pieces. Melt the butter in a large skillet and cook the chicken pieces until they are brown all over. Remove the chicken pieces from the skillet and drain on paper towels. Put the baby white onions and bacon in the skillet and cook until softened. Add the flour and cook, stirring, for 2–3 minutes. Then add the mushrooms, wine, broth, bouquet garni, salt and pepper. Bring to a boil, then lower the heat, return chicken, cover, and simmer for 35–45 minutes, or until the chicken is tender.

Remove the bouquet garni. Serve the chicken in a heated dish with the sauce poured over it.

Chicken cacciatore

Chicken cacciatore

Serves 4

1 boiler/fryer, about 3 lb
all-purpose flour, for coating
$\frac{1}{4}$ cup ($\frac{1}{2}$ stick) butter
1 tablespoon olive oil
1 large onion, chopped
2 garlic cloves, chopped
8 tomatoes, peeled and chopped
3 tablespoons concentrated tomato paste
1 teaspoon sugar
$\frac{3}{4}$ cup chicken broth
salt and pepper
2 cups sliced button mushrooms
4 tablespoons Marsala wine or sweet vermouth
boiled pasta shapes, to serve

Cut the chicken into pieces and coat with flour. Heat the butter and olive oil together in a large skillet. Add the chicken and cook until crisp and golden all over. Remove and keep hot. Add the onion and garlic to the skillet and cook gently until pale gold. Stir in the tomatoes, tomato paste, sugar and broth, then season well with salt and pepper. Bring to a boil, then replace the chicken. Reduce the heat, cover the skillet and simmer slowly for 30–45 minutes. Add the mushrooms and wine or vermouth and continue to cook for 10–15 minutes. Serve with boiled pasta shapes.

Italian-style chicken in wine
Serves 4

1 boiler/fryer, about 4 lb
all-purpose flour, for coating
salt and pepper
$\frac{1}{4}$ cup ($\frac{1}{2}$ stick) butter
$\frac{1}{4}$ cup olive oil
1 medium-sized onion, chopped
2 medium-sized carrots, pared and thinly sliced
2 celery stalks, thinly sliced
8–10 chopped chicken livers
$\frac{1}{2}$ cup chicken broth
$\frac{3}{4}$ cup dry red wine
1 teaspoon dried basil
1 cup sliced mushrooms
2 teaspoons finely chopped parsley
3 tablespoons Marsala wine or other sweet red wine
watercress, to garnish

Cut the chicken into pieces and coat with flour seasoned with a little salt and pepper. Heat the butter and olive oil together in a large skillet. Add the chicken and cook until golden brown all over. Remove the chicken from the skillet and keep hot. Add the onion, carrots, celery and chicken livers to the butter and oil remaining in the skillet and cook slowly until the onion is golden. Add the broth, wine, basil and mushrooms, then replace the chicken pieces. Cover and cook gently for 30 minutes. Then add seasoning, parsley and wine and continue to simmer until the chicken is tender. Garnish with watercress. Serve with boiled pasta or buttered potatoes and a green salad.

Above: Italian-style chicken in wine
Opposite top: Old English chicken pie
Opposite bottom: Chicken and pear vol-au-vents

Chicken and pear vol-au-vents
Serves 4

1 package (17¼ oz) frozen puff pastry, thawed
1 egg, beaten
2 cups cold cooked chicken
1 egg yolk
1¼ cups béchamel sauce
juice of ½ lemon
1 lb pears
¼ teaspoon ground nutmeg
salt and pepper

Preheat the oven to 475°. Roll out the pastry on a lightly floured board to ½-inch thick. Cut it into four circles about 2-inches in diameter. Mark another circle in the center of each circle, using a smaller cookie cutter, but cut only halfway through the pastry. Mark a criss-cross pattern in the center circle with a knife. Leave the pastry in a cool place for 20 minutes before baking. Brush the tops with beaten egg, then bake 10 minutes. Reduce temperature to 375° for a further 10–15 minutes, or until cooked.

Meanwhile, cut the chicken into bite-sized pieces. Add the egg yolk to the béchamel sauce and reheat without boiling. Stir in the chicken and lemon juice. Pare, core and chop the pears and add them to the sauce. Reheat and season with nutmeg, and salt and pepper.

Remove the center circle from each vol-au-vent shell, taking care not to break it. Scoop out the pastry in the middle and spoon in the sauce. Replace the lid. Serve immediately.

Old English chicken pie
Serves 6

1 cup packaged sage and onion stuffing mix
2 cups diced raw chicken
½ cup all-purpose flour
salt and pepper
¼ cup (½ stick) butter
¼ lb sausagemeat
2 cups chicken broth
2 eggs, hard-boiled and chopped
1 package (2 sticks) pie crust pastry
1 egg, to glaze

Prepare the stuffing mix and form it into small balls. Toss the chicken in half the flour mixed with a little seasoning. Melt the butter in a skillet and brown the stuffing balls, chicken and sausagemeat. Then remove from the skillet and put in a square ovenproof baking dish. Stir the remaining flour into any fat remaining in the skillet, cook 2 minutes, then gradually stir in the broth. Bring to a boil and cook until thickened, stirring constantly. Add the hard-boiled eggs to the sauce and pour it over the chicken, sausagemeat and stuffing balls. Allow to cool slightly.

Preheat the oven to 425°. Roll out the pastry to ¼-inch thickness to cover the baking dish. From the trimmings, make a strip of dough to go around the moistened edge of the baking dish. Brush the rim of pastry with a little water. Place the pastry over the baking dish, using a rolling pin to ease it over. Press the edges together, cut away any surplus and flute the edge with a knife. Cut a slit in the top and decorate with leaves made from the trimmings.

Bake in the center of the oven about 20 minutes or until the pastry is golden brown. Then reduce the heat to 350° and bake for a further 20 minutes. Serve hot.

Crispy game hens with green peppers
Serves 4

2 Rock Cornish Game Hens
1 garlic clove
juice of $\frac{1}{2}$ lemon
all-purpose flour, for coating
salt and pepper
$\frac{1}{4}$ cup ($\frac{1}{2}$ stick) butter
$\frac{1}{4}$ cup olive oil
1 medium-sized onion, sliced
1 green pepper, seeded, sliced and coarsely chopped
$\frac{1}{2}$ teaspoon dried rosemary
$\frac{1}{4}$ cup red wine
lemon slices, to garnish

Cut each rock Cornish game hen into halves or quarters, depending on size. Rub them with a cut garlic clove and sprinkle with lemon juice. Dust the pieces lightly with well-seasoned flour.

Heat the butter and olive oil together in a large skillet. Add the pieces of game hen, skin side up, and cook until golden, then turn and cook the other side. Remove from the skillet and keep hot. Cook the onion and green pepper in the butter and oil remaining in the skillet. After a few minutes, add the rosemary and wine. Then return the Cornish game hen pieces to the skillet, cover, and continue cooking until tender. Garnish with lemon slices.

Chicken terrine

Serves 4 to 6

1 boiler/fryer, about 3½ lb
½ lb lean pork or veal tenderloin
12 bacon slices
salt and pepper
½ lb pork sausagemeat
¼ cup strong chicken broth
1 tablespoon freshly chopped parsley

Remove the skin from the chicken and cut the breast meat into neat slices. Remove the rest of the chicken meat from the bones and grind it with the pork or veal and two bacon slices. Season the ground meat well and mix it with the sausagemeat and half the broth.

Line the bottom of an oval or oblong ovenproof dish with half the remaining bacon slices. Put a layer of the ground meat over the slices. Then add some of the sliced chicken breast, sprinkle it lightly with stock and chopped parsley. Continue filling the dish like this, ending with ground meat. Cover with the remaining bacon slices. Cover with a well-fitting lid or foil.

Preheat the oven to 325°. Stand the dish in a baking pan of cold water and cook in the center of the oven for 1½ hours. Remove the lid or foil and put a light weight (about 2 lb) over the terrine so that it is pressed into a neat shape as it cools. Turn out when cold and serve cut into thin slices.

Opposite top: Crispy game hens with green peppers
Opposite bottom: Chicken in red wine
Above: Chicken terrine

Chicken in red wine

Serves 4

1 boiler/fryer, about 3 lb
6 tablespoons butter
8 baby white onions
4 slices bacon, diced
3 tablespoons brandy
1¼ cups chicken broth
2½ cups red wine
salt and freshly ground black pepper
bouquet garni
2 garlic cloves, crushed
1 cup button mushrooms
¼ cup all-purpose flour
To garnish
finely chopped fresh parsley
croutons of fried bread

Cut the chicken into four pieces. Melt 4 tablespoons butter in a large skillet and cook the chicken until golden, then remove it and drain on paper towels. Then cook the onions and bacon in the skillet until golden, stirring occasionally. Return the chicken to the skillet, pour in the brandy and set light to it. When the flames have died down add the broth, wine, salt, pepper, bouquet garni, garlic and mushrooms. Bring to a boil, then reduce the heat, cover and simmer for 35-45 minutes or until the chicken is tender.

Remove the chicken pieces from the skillet and discard the bouquet garni. Place the chicken on a heated serving dish and keep hot. Mix the remaining butter with the flour to make a smooth paste. Bring the cooking liquid to a boil and add the butter and flour mixture in small pieces, stirring constantly, until the sauce has thickened. Allow the sauce to boil for 2–3 minutes.

Pour the sauce over the chicken, sprinkle with chopped parsley and arrange the croutons around the edge of the dish. Serve very hot.

Dry chicken curry with yellow rice
Serves 4

Indian curry dishes are made from a blend of exotic, strong and often very hot spices. Because many of these spices are not easily available it is an acceptable alternative to use a prepared curry powder. Madras, the combination recommended in this recipe, is very hot and spicy. Korma is a much milder powder and – for the very adventurous – vindaloo is the hottest.

3 tablespoons butter
1 large onion, finely chopped
1 green pepper, seeded, sliced and diced
1 garlic clove, crushed
1 tablespoon Madras curry powder, or a milder curry powder to suit your taste
1 teaspoon chili powder
salt
4 chicken pieces
4 medium-sized tomatoes
2 tablespoons plain yogurt
For the rice
2 tablespoons butter
1½ cups long grain rice
1 teaspoon ground turmeric
few cloves
1 teaspoon ground cumin
salt
2½ cups water
thinly sliced cucumber, to garnish

Melt the butter in a skillet and cook the onion, pepper and garlic for about 5 minutes. Add the curry powder, chili powder and a pinch of salt; mix well. Put the chicken pieces in the skillet and brown quickly over high heat. Then lower the heat, cover and simmer gently for 1 hour. If the chicken pieces are fresh, add 2–3 tablespoons of water before lowering the heat. (If the chicken pieces are frozen they probably will not need water.) Add the whole tomatoes to the skillet 5 minutes before the end of the cooking time. Stir in the yogurt just before serving.

While the chicken is cooking, prepare the rice: heat the butter in a saucepan and toss the rice in it for 5 minutes. Add the spices and a pinch of salt and mix well. Pour in the water, bring to a boil, then cover and simmer gently for 15 minutes or until the rice is tender and all the liquid absorbed.

Italian fried chicken
Serves 4

8 chicken drumsticks, thawed if frozen
1 tablespoon all-purpose flour
salt and pepper
1 large egg, beaten
1 cup dry bread crumbs
2 tablespoons grated Parmesan cheese
vegetable oil, for frying
watercress, to garnish
For the rice mixture
$\frac{1}{4}$ cup ($\frac{1}{2}$ stick) butter
1 green pepper, seeded, sliced and diced
1 red pepper, seeded, sliced and diced
$1\frac{1}{3}$ cups long grain rice
$2\frac{1}{2}$ cups chicken broth
salt and pepper
1 cup cooked peas
$\frac{1}{2}$ cup canned whole kernel corn, drained

Coat the drumsticks with seasoned flour, then with beaten egg and the bread crumbs mixed with the grated cheese. If possible, chill for a while so that the coating sets.

Melt the butter in a saucepan and cook the peppers for a few minutes. Add the rice and stir it in the butter until the grains are transparent. Add the broth and bring to a boil, stirring. Season well and cook until the rice is nearly tender, then add the peas and whole kernel corn. Continue cooking until the rice is tender and all the liquid is absorbed.

Meanwhile, deep fry the chicken drumsticks in the hot vegetable oil. Take care that the oil is not too hot, otherwise the cheese will scorch. Drain the drumsticks on paper towels. Pile the rice mixture onto a hot dish and arrange the drumsticks around it. Garnish with sprigs of watercress.

Roast stuffed duck with orange sauce
Serves 5 to 6

1 duck about 4–5 lb
salt and pepper
1 garlic clove
juice of 1 orange
For the stuffing
2 tablespoons chicken fat
1 small onion, chopped
$\frac{1}{3}$ cup raisins, soaked in 2 tablespoons hot broth
4 cups cooked long grain rice
1 apple, pared and chopped
For the orange sauce
1 tablespoon all-purpose flour
juice and rind of 1 orange
juice and rind of $\frac{1}{2}$ lemon
$\frac{3}{4}$ cup broth
salt and pepper

Melt the fat for the stuffing in a skillet and cook the onion. Mix in the raisins, rice, apple and seasoning.

Preheat the oven to 425°. Season the duck with salt and pepper and rub the outside with the cut clove of garlic. Stuff the bird and place it on a wire rack in a baking pan. Pour the orange juice over and cover the breast with aluminum foil. Cook. After 15 minutes, turn the oven down to 375°. Remove the foil 30 minutes before the end of the cooking time ($1\frac{1}{2}$–2 hours, according to size).

Remove the duck from the oven and keep it hot. Pour off the fat except for 1 tablespoon. Add the flour for the sauce and cook until brown. Add the juice and rind of 1 orange and $\frac{1}{2}$ lemon and the broth. Cook until thick, stirring continually. Adjust seasoning and strain the sauce into a sauce boat.

Note: Broth can be made by boiling the giblets, onion and seasoning.

Roast duck with Marsala wine
Serves 4

2 fresh sage leaves, or $\frac{1}{4}$ teaspoon dried sage
1 garlic clove, halved
1 duck, about 4 lb
salt and pepper
$\frac{1}{2}$ cup Marsala wine

Preheat the oven to 375°. Put the sage and garlic in the body cavity of the duck and place it on a wire rack in a large baking pan. Prick the skin all over with a fork, then sprinkle with salt and pepper. Pour the Marsala wine into the pan. Roast in the center of the oven for $1\frac{1}{2}$ hours, basting at least twice.

Duck casserole
Serves 4

1 duck, about 4 lb
12 baby white onions
1 garlic clove, crushed
4 carrots, pared and halved or quartered
2 cups duck broth (made from the giblets)
salt and pepper
$\frac{1}{4}$ cup all-purpose flour
4 large potatoes, coarsely sliced
parsley sprig, to garnish
For the sage and onion stuffing
2 large onions, chopped
$\frac{3}{4}$ cup water
salt and pepper
1 cup soft white bread crumbs
1–2 teaspoons chopped fresh sage, or $\frac{1}{2}$ teaspoon dried sage
$\frac{1}{4}$ cup margarine, melted
1 egg

Preheat the oven to 425°–450°. First make the stuffing: Cook the onions for 10 minutes in the water and season well. Strain, then blend the onion with the bread crumbs, sage and margarine. Bind with the egg. Place the stuffing in the cavity of the duck and roast about 30 minutes, or until the skin is crisp and brown and much of the fat has run out.

While the duck is cooking, simmer the onions, garlic and carrots in $1\frac{1}{4}$ cups of the broth for 30 minutes; season well. Blend the flour with the remaining broth, stir it into the vegetables and cook until there is a smooth, thickened sauce. Transfer the vegetables and sauce to an ovenproof casserole and put in the potatoes.

Reduce the oven to 350°. Place the duck on top of the vegetables, cover and cook $1\frac{1}{2}$ hours in the center of the oven. Garnish with parsley sprigs.

Creamed turkey duchesse
Serves 4 to 6

2 cups cooled mashed potatoes
2 eggs, or 2 egg yolks
$\frac{1}{4}$ cup ($\frac{1}{2}$ stick) butter
salt and pepper
1 cup button mushrooms
1 green pepper, seeded, sliced and diced
$1\frac{1}{4}$ cups broth
$\frac{1}{4}$ cup all-purpose flour
$\frac{1}{2}$ cup milk
few drops of hot-pepper sauce
2 cups diced cooked turkey
2–3 tablespoons light cream
chopped parsley, to garnish

Preheat the oven to 350°. Mix the mashed potatoes with 1 egg or egg yolk and half the butter; season well. Form the potato into a border around an ovenproof dish. Brush with the second egg or egg yolk, diluted with a few drops of water, and brown in the oven.

Meanwhile, simmer the whole mushrooms and diced green pepper in the broth for 10 minutes. Strain off the liquid and put it aside for the sauce.

Heat the remainder of the butter in a saucepan, stir in the flour and cook for 2 minutes, stirring. Gradually stir in the milk, then the broth. Bring to a boil and cook until the sauce thickens, stirring constantly. Season well and flavor with hot-pepper sauce. Put the vegetables and turkey in the sauce and heat gently for a few minutes. Stir in the cream. Put the turkey mixture inside the potato border and garnish with parsley.

Opposite top left: Roast stuffed duck
with orange sauce (recipe on previous page)
Opposite top right: Duck casserole
Opposite bottom: Roast duck with Marsala wine
Above right: Creamed turkey duchesse

Roast turkey with stuffing

Serves 14

1 turkey, about 12 lb
several slices bacon, to cover the bird's breast
For the stuffing
1 cup chopped lean ham
$\frac{1}{2}$ lb sausagemeat
1 teaspoon chopped parsley
grated rind of 1 lemon
$\frac{1}{3}$ cup golden raisins
1 egg, beaten
salt and pepper
To garnish
8 bacon slices
1 lb cocktail sausages
watercress sprig
For the gravy
1–2 tablespoons all-purpose flour
$1\frac{1}{4}$–$2\frac{1}{2}$ cups broth (made from the giblets)

Roast turkey with stuffing

Combine all the ingredients for the stuffing and season well. Lift the skin of the neck of the turkey and place stuffing under it. Pull the skin gently over the stuffing and fasten it with a skewer. Put any remaining stuffing inside the bird. Cross the legs over the opening and secure them with kitchen string. Weigh the bird to calculate the cooking time (see below). Cover the bird's breast with the bacon.

Preheat the oven to 425°–450°. Place the turkey in a roasting pan. Place in oven and baste frequently. After 30 minutes reduce heat to 350°–375°.

To make the garnish, cut the bacon slices in half. Stretch each slice with the blunt edge of a knife, then roll up and secure with a wooden toothpick or metal skewer. Broil the bacon rolls and cocktail sausages and place around the cooked turkey. Garnish with watercress.

Make the gravy with the flour, broth and juices in the roasting pan. Serve with cranberry sauce.

To calculate cooking time: Allow 15 minutes per 1 lb and 15 minutes over for a bird up to 12 lb in weight. After that, add 12 minutes per 1 lb up to 21 lb. Above that weight, allow only 10 more minutes for each additional 1 lb. If the bird is exceptionally broad breasted, allow a little extra time.

Roast pheasants

Serves 8

$\frac{1}{4}$ cup ($\frac{1}{2}$ stick) butter
2 young pheasants
2 slices bacon
salt and pepper
For the gravy
1 tablespoon all-purpose flour
$1\frac{1}{4}$ cups broth (made from the giblets)
To garnish
1 cup button mushrooms
2 tablespoons butter

Preheat the oven to 425°–450°. Place a small knob of butter inside each bird and truss. Melt the rest of the butter in a roasting pan, place the birds in the pan and spoon the butter over them. Lay the bacon slices over the top of the birds. Put the pheasants in the oven and roast for 15 minutes. Lower the heat to 350°–375° and roast for a further 30–35 minutes or until tender. Baste from time to time to keep the birds moist.

Make the gravy: Pour off the grease from the roasting pan. Mix the flour with the juices left in the pan and cook for 2 minutes. Then stir in the broth, bring to a boil and cook until thickened, stirring well. Add a little salt and pepper and strain the gravy.

Serve garnished with button mushrooms cooked in butter, if wished. Traditional accompaniments for pheasant are fried bread crumbs, bread sauce and game chips.

Above: Roast goose; Below: Roast pheasants

Roast goose
Serves 6 to 8

1 goose, about 12 lb
1 tablespoon all-purpose flour
1¼ cups broth, made from the giblets
apple sauce, to serve
For sage and onion stuffing
2 large onions, finely chopped
½ cup water
salt and pepper
1 cup fresh white bread crumbs
1 teaspoon chopped fresh sage, or ½ teaspoon dried sage
¼ cup melted margarine
1 egg, beaten

Preheat the oven to 425°–450°. As goose is very fatty, no extra fat is needed for cooking: place the bird on a wire rack in the roasting pan to allow the fat to drain off. To make the stuffing, cook the onions in the water for 10 minutes, then strain and season well. Save a little of the water for the stuffing. Combine all the ingredients, using just enough egg to bind the stuffing and moisten with a little of the onion water. Place the stuffing inside the goose and truss. Roast in the oven. After 30 minutes reduce the heat to 350°. Allow 15 minutes per 1 lb and 15 minutes over. Prick the goose all over with a fork two or three times during cooking to allow the fat to run out.

Make gravy with the flour, juices in the pan and the broth. Serve with apple sauce.

Variation: You can vary the stuffing ingredients in this dish quite easily – for instance, substitute apples for the onions, or replace sage with chopped mint or parsley.

Hare in Madeira sauce
Serves 4

Above: Hare in Madeira sauce
Opposite: Landè-style jugged hare

4 pieces of young hare
1 tablespoon all-purpose flour
½ teaspoon chopped sage
½ cup (1 stick) butter
1 cup button mushrooms
1 cup Madeira wine
½ teaspoon chopped fresh herbs, or good pinch of dried herbs
salt and pepper

Preheat the oven to 375°–400°. Sprinkle the hare pieces with the flour mixed with the sage. Melt half the butter in a skillet and cook the hare until brown. Lift the pieces out of the skillet and put them in an ovenproof casserole. Heat the rest of the butter and cook the mushrooms in it. Add the mushrooms to the casserole with the wine, herbs and seasoning. Cover the casserole and cook for 1 hour.

Landè-style jugged hare

Serves 6

1 hare
$\frac{1}{4}$ cup pork fat or shortening
10 scallions
2 garlic cloves, crushed
$\frac{1}{4}$ lb ham, diced
$\frac{3}{4}$ cup red wine
1 cup water
4 tomatoes, peeled, seeded and chopped
$\frac{1}{2}$ cup button mushrooms
salt and freshly ground black pepper
croutons, to garnish

Cut the hare into serving pieces. Heat the pork fat in a large skillet and cook the hare until browned all over. Remove the hare, drain it on paper towels and place it in an ovenproof casserole. Brown the scallions and add them to the casserole with the remaining ingredients, except the croutons.

Preheat the oven to 325°. Cover the casserole tightly and cook for $1\frac{1}{2}$–2 hours, or until the hare is very tender. Place the hare, ham and vegetables on a heated serving dish. Strain the sauce into a pan, bring to a boil and boil rapidly until it has thickened slightly.

Pour the sauce over the hare and garnish with croutons, arranged around the edge of the dish.

Vegetarian dishes

Cauliflower surprise
Serves 4 to 6

$\frac{1}{2}$ cup (1 stick) butter
2 medium-sized onions, peeled and sliced
2 tomatoes, peeled and sliced
6 mushrooms, sliced
1 can (7 oz) whole kernel corn, drained
$\frac{1}{4}$ cup cooked peas
1 medium-sized cauliflower
salt and pepper
$\frac{1}{2}$ cup all-purpose flour
2 cups milk
1 cup finely grated cheese

Melt half the butter in a saucepan and cook the onions, tomatoes and mushrooms until tender. Add the whole kernel corn and peas. Heat gently and keep hot. Meanwhile, cook the whole cauliflower in boiling salted water until just tender.

Melt the remaining butter in a skillet, stir in the flour and cook for 2 minutes. Gradually blend in the milk and $\frac{3}{4}$ cup water from the cauliflower and cook until the sauce has thickened, stirring constantly. Mix half the sauce with the vegetable mixture and put it in the bottom of a hot, deep flameproof serving dish or casserole. Put the cauliflower on top. Add the grated cheese to the remaining sauce and spoon it over the cauliflower. Brown under the broiler and serve at once.

Savory vegetable strudel

Serves 4 to 6

1½ cups all-purpose flour
½ cup butter or margarine, well chilled
½ cup water, plus 2 tablespoons
1 teaspoon vinegar

For the filling

2 tablespoons vegetable oil
2 medium-sized onions, chopped
1 cup chopped mushrooms
2 tomatoes, peeled and chopped
¾ lb frozen spinach
1 tablespoon chopped nuts or sesame seeds
½ teaspoon salt
pinch of pepper
pinch of dried mixed herbs
pinch of garlic salt
1 tablespoon finely chopped parsley

For the topping

1½ tablespoons butter, melted
¼ cup dry bread crumbs
extra nuts or sesame seeds

First make the pastry: Sift the flour into a bowl and add the butter or margarine cut into large pieces. Mix with water and vinegar, adding enough to make a soft dough. Roll out the dough into an oblong and fold it in three, then seal the edges and turn to the left. Repeat this procedure twice, then refrigerate.

To make the filling, heat the oil in a skillet and cook the onions until a pale brown. Add the mushrooms, tomatoes and spinach. Add the rest of the filling ingredients and cook for about 10 minutes or until the spinach is cooked and liquid has evaporated. Leave the mixture to cool.

Preheat the oven to 425°. Cut the dough in two, roll it out thinly into an oblong and brush with one-third of the melted butter and half the bread crumbs. Spread half the filling to within 1 inch of the edge of the dough. Wet the edges, roll up, brush with melted butter and sprinkle with nuts or sesame seeds. Repeat with the rest of the dough and filling. Place on a greased baking sheet and cook 30 minutes, or until brown.

Opposite: Cauliflower surprise
Below: Savory vegetable strudel

Rice and vegetable casserole
Serves 4 to 6

Above left: Rice and vegetable casserole
Above right: Vegetable casserole
Opposite: Cabbage and tomato casserole

1 medium-sized onion, chopped
2 garlic cloves, chopped
1 green pepper, seeded, sliced and chopped
3 tablespoons olive oil
3 carrots, pared and diced
$\frac{1}{2}$ lb young green beans, chopped
1 can (about 8 oz) kidney beans, drained
1 tablespoon chopped parsley
1 lb rice, partly cooked
$3\frac{3}{4}$ cups vegetable broth
$\frac{1}{4}$ teaspoon saffron
$\frac{1}{4}$ teaspoon turmeric
$\frac{1}{4}$ teaspoon crushed coriander

Cook the onion, garlic and pepper gently in olive oil until soft. Add all the vegetables, parsley and rice and stir. Heat the vegetable broth and stir in the saffron, turmeric and coriander. Add the liquid slowly to the rice mixture. Bring to a boil, reduce heat, cover and cook gently until all the liquid is absorbed, about 20 minutes. Serve hot.

Vegetable casserole
Serves 4

2 large onions, coarsely chopped
2 garlic cloves, chopped
vegetable oil, for frying
2 green peppers, seeded, sliced and chopped
4 zucchini, sliced and salted
2 medium-sized eggplant, sliced, salted and drained
2 cups sliced mushrooms
1 lb ripe tomatoes, peeled and chopped
1 can (about 2 oz) concentrated tomato paste
2 bay leaves
1 tablespoon finely chopped parsley
$\frac{1}{2}$ teaspoon dried oregano
$\frac{1}{2}$ teaspoon dried thyme
2 large potatoes, pared and thinly sliced
wheatgerm (optional)
2 tablespoons butter or margarine

Cook the onions and garlic in oil in a large heavy-bottomed skillet. Add peppers, zucchini, eggplant and mushrooms and cook for a few minutes. Then tip the vegetables into a deep ovenproof casserole and add the tomatoes, tomato paste and the herbs. Top with a layer of potato slices and sprinkle with wheatgerm if liked. Preheat oven to 350°. Dot with butter or margarine and bake in the oven for about 1 hour, or until the potatoes are soft underneath and crisp and brown on top. Serve hot.

Cabbage and tomato casserole
Serves 4

$\frac{1}{4}$ cup ($\frac{1}{2}$ stick) butter
1 medium-sized onion, grated
1 small apple, grated
4 large tomatoes, peeled and chopped
$\frac{1}{2}$ cup water, plus 2 tablespoons
salt and pepper
$\frac{1}{2}$ small head cabbage, shredded and cooked
1 cup finely grated Cheddar cheese
$\frac{1}{2}$ cup dry bread crumbs

Melt the butter in a large skillet and gently cook the onion, apple and tomatoes. Add the water and seasoning and simmer to a thick purée. Add the cabbage and heat through. Put in a heatproof dish, sprinkle with the cheese and crumbs and brown under the broiler.

For a variation, use cauliflower or thickly sliced potato instead of cabbage.

Chick-pea casserole
Serves 4 to 6

½ lb chick-peas, soaked overnight and drained
1 garlic clove, chopped
1 medium-sized onion, chopped
4 large tomatoes, peeled and chopped
1 small head cabbage, shredded
½ green pepper, seeded, sliced and chopped
4 tablespoons vegetable oil
½ teaspoon ground ginger
pinch of ground cloves
1 teaspoon salt
freshly ground black pepper
½ cup water or vegetable broth

Simmer the chick-peas in water for 1½–3 hours, or until tender. Cook the garlic and vegetables in oil and season with ginger, cloves, salt and pepper. Add the drained chick-peas to the vegetables and pour in the water or broth.

Preheat the oven to 350°. Place the ingredients in a buttered ovenproof casserole and cook 20–30 minutes. Serve hot.

Lentil rissoles
Serves 6

½ cup brown or yellow lentils, soaked overnight and drained
1 large onion, grated
2 medium-sized potatoes, pared, boiled and mashed
1 cup fresh bread crumbs
1 cup chopped almonds
2 tablespoons sesame seeds
sea salt
2 tablespoons chopped parsley
1 egg, beaten

Bring lentils to a boil in a saucepan of cold salted water. Cover and simmer until they are tender, about 1¼ hours. Then drain and mash them and mix with the onion, potatoes, bread crumbs, nuts, sesame seeds, salt, parsley and egg. Add enough cold water to bind the mixture together.

Preheat the oven to 350°. Form into rissoles, place on a greased baking sheet and bake in the oven for 25 minutes. If preferred, cook them gently in oil for 15 minutes, or until golden on both sides, turning once. Serve hot with a green vegetable or green salad and tomato sauce.

Broiled cheese-spinach
Serves 4

2 lb fresh spinach, or about ¾ lb frozen spinach

salt and pepper

½ cup (1 stick) butter

3 tablespoons heavy cream

4 large tomatoes, peeled and chopped

2 medium-sized onions, chopped

1 cup grated Cheddar or other hard cheese

4 hard-boiled eggs (optional)

Wash the fresh spinach well and cook in the water clinging to the leaves in a covered pan over gentle heat; add a little salt. Cook frozen spinach as directed on the package. Drain the spinach and press out the excess water in a strainer and chop finely. Return it to the saucepan with half the butter and the cream. Heat gently to a creamy consistency. Add pepper to taste.

While the spinach is cooking, heat the tomatoes and onions in the remaining butter until soft. Add the cheese and season. Put the creamed spinach in a shallow heatproof dish, put the hard-boiled eggs on top, if using, then cover with the tomato mixture. Heat for a few minutes under the broiler and serve immediately.

Opposite left: Chick pea casserole
Above: Lentil rissoles
Below: Broiled cheese-spinach

Light meals, picnics & barbecues

Barbecued chicken drumsticks
Serves 6

2 tablespoons butter, melted
1 tablespoon mustard
few drops Worcestershire or chili sauce
6 chicken drumsticks

Mix the melted butter with the mustard and Worcestershire or chili sauce and brush the chicken drumsticks with it. Barbecue over hot coals, turning occasionally, until cooked through. The drumsticks are cooked when the juices turn clear when they are pricked in the thickest part. Serve with barbecued sausages and barbecue sauce.

Barbecued beef saté

Serves 4

2 lb top round steak, cut into 1-inch cubes
2 tablespoons soy sauce
1 tablespoon clear honey
2 garlic cloves, crushed
1 teaspoon ground coriander
1 teaspoon caraway seeds
$\frac{1}{4}$ teaspoon chili powder
2 tablespoons vegetable oil

Place the steak in a large bowl. Mix the remaining ingredients and pour over the meat. Marinate the steak for 1 hour, stirring occasionally. Thread the meat onto six skewers. Barbecue over hot coals, turning occasionally, for 10 minutes or until cooked to taste. Baste with the marinade during cooking. Serve with barbecue sauce.

Barbecue sauce

Makes about 2 cups

2 medium-sized onions, finely chopped
2 tablespoons light brown sugar
2 tablespoons lime or lemon juice
1 tablespoon soy sauce
$\frac{1}{2}$ cup water
$\frac{1}{2}$ cup concentrated tomato paste
freshly ground black pepper

Place all the ingredients, except the pepper, in a saucepan and heat gently, stirring constantly, until the sugar is dissolved. Add pepper to taste.

Opposite: Barbecued chicken drumsticks
Right: Barbecued beef saté with barbecue sauce

Picnic
Mixed cold meats
Green mayonnaise
Salad niçoise
Potato salad
Stuffed French loaf
Fruit and cheese
Serves 4 to 6

Green mayonnaise

1 tablespoon finely chopped fresh parsley
1 tablespoon finely chopped fresh mint
$\frac{1}{4}$ teaspoon finely chopped fresh tarragon
$\frac{1}{4}$ teaspoon finely chopped fresh thyme
$\frac{3}{4}$ cup thick mayonnaise

Mix the chopped herbs with the mayonnaise. Use half the mayonnaise for the potato salad and put the rest in a screw-top jar to serve with the Mixed cold meats.

Potato salad

Mix about 2 cups diced cooked potatoes with a little bottled oil and vinegar salad dressing, then with half the Green Mayonnaise. Sprinkle over 2 tablespoons chopped chives, scallions, or grated onion.

Salad niçoise

1 head lettuce
3 tomatoes
2 hard-boiled eggs, sliced
2 cups cooked new potatoes, sliced (optional)
$\frac{1}{2}$ lb cooked green beans
1 can (7 oz) tuna, drained and flaked
1 can (2 oz) anchovy fillets, drained and separated
mayonnaise or bottled oil and vinegar dressing
salt and pepper
black olives, to garnish

Make a salad of the lettuce, tomatoes and eggs. Add the potatoes, if using and beans. Then add the tuna and anchovy fillets and toss in mayonnaise or oil and vinegar dressing. Add extra seasoning if required. Garnish with black olives.

To take the salad on a picnic, pack the lettuce, tomatoes, eggs, potatoes and cooked beans in a plastic box. Leave the tuna and anchovy fillets in cans, put the dressing in a screw-top jar and pack the olives separately. Assemble the salad just before eating. Serve with hunks of French bread.

Stuffed French loaf

For each French loaf
$\frac{1}{4}$ cup ($\frac{1}{2}$ stick) butter
1–2 teaspoons French-style mustard
2 tablespoons tomato catsup
1 tablespoon chopped dill pickle
1–2 tablespoons chopped scallions or chives
$\frac{3}{4}$ lb liver sausage or cooked ground beef

Cream the butter and mix it with all the other ingredients. Split the loaf lengthwise and spread thinly with butter. Spread on the filling and reshape the loaf. Wrap the loaf in foil to take it to the picnic, or pack the filling, butter and loaf separately and put together just before eating.

Haddock charlotte with
Creamed carrots and
Duchessse potatoes
Peach madrilènes
Serves 4

Haddock charlotte
Serves 4

1¼ lb cooked and flaked haddock steaks

1 egg, beaten

¾ cup milk

salt and pepper

1 teaspoon finely grated lemon rind

1 teaspoon finely chopped parsley

4–5 large slices bread, crusts removed and buttered

To garnish

tomato slices

lemon wedges

Preheat the oven to 350°. Mix the flaked fish with the egg, milk, seasoning, lemon rind and parsley. Cut the bread into thin strips and cover the bottom of a 2-pint oval baking dish with a layer of bread, buttered side down. Spoon the fish mixture over the bread and top with a layer of bread fingers, buttered side up. Bake in the center of the oven until the topping is crisp. Garnish with tomato slices and lemon wedges.

Creamed carrots
Serves 4

1 lb carrots, pared and sliced

1 tablespoon butter

2 tablespoons light cream

chopped parsley, to garnish

Cook the carrots until tender, then mash well. Mix mashed carrots with the butter and cream and pile into a serving dish. Garnish with chopped parsley.

Duchesse potatoes
Serves 4

1½ lb potatoes, pared and chopped

¼ cup (½ stick) butter

1 or 2 egg yolks

Cook and mash the potatoes, then strain them to remove any lumps. Beat the butter and the egg yolks into the mashed potato. Do not add milk as it makes the potato shapes spread out. Pipe the potatoes into rose shapes, or pile in pyramid shapes, on to a greased cookie sheet. Heat through and brown in the oven with the haddock charlotte.

Peach madrilènes
Serves 4

1 orange, divided into segments

¾ cup heavy cream

superfine sugar

12 grapes, halved and seeded

2 large peaches or 4 small ones, halved and pitted

**Harlequin soufflé omelet
with broccoli
Hot melon with ginger**
Serves 4

Harlequin soufflé omelet
Serves 4

8 eggs, separated
2 cups cottage cheese, strained
salt and pepper
1 tablespoon chopped parsley
2 tablespoons chopped chives or scallions
$\frac{1}{4}$ cup ($\frac{1}{2}$ stick) butter
To garnish
1 red pepper, seeded and sliced
1 green pepper, seeded and sliced

Beat the egg yolks with the cottage cheese and seasoning until smooth. Add the parsley and chives or scallions. Then fold in the stiffly beaten egg whites.

Melt the butter in a very large skillet (or make two omelets in a smaller skillet). Pour in the egg mixture and cook steadily for about 5 minutes, until the underside is golden. Then cook under a medium broiler for 3–4 minutes, until set. Slide the omelet out of the skillet onto a hot dish (do not fold). Garnish with pepper rings and serve at once.

Remove the skin, pith and pits from the orange segments and cut the fruit into neat pieces. Whip the cream until it just holds its shape and sweeten. Add the grapes and orange segments and pile the mixture into the peach halves.

For variation, thick smooth custard, dairy soured cream or plain yogurt may be used in place of the cream.

Broccoli
Serves 4

1½ lb broccoli

2 tablespoons butter, melted

salt and pepper

Cook the broccoli in boiling salted water, or steam it, until tender, about 10–12 minutes. Toss the broccoli in melted butter and place it in a serving dish. Season.

Hot melon with ginger
Serves 4

1 ripe honeydew melon, sliced and seeded

juice of ½ orange

little ground ginger

Preheat the oven to 350°. Moisten the melon slices with the orange juice and sprinkle with a little ground ginger. Warm the melon in the oven for about 20 minutes. Serve hot.

Broccoli and Hot melon with ginger

**Tomato juice cocktail
Savoury cheese log with
Garlic bread and salad
Pineapple soufflé
dessert**
Serves 4 to 6

Tomato juice cocktail
Serves 4 to 6

2½ cups tomato juice

shake of celery salt

pinch of cayenne

little Worcestershire sauce

finely chopped mint leaves

To decorate glasses

1 egg white, lightly beaten

very finely chopped mint or parsley

Mix the tomato juice with the seasoning, Worcestershire sauce and mint leaves. Chill.

To decorate the glasses, dip the rims in beaten egg white, then in the chopped mint or parsley.

Savory cheese log
Serves 4 to 6

4 cups finely grated Cheddar or other hard cheese

2 tablespoons each of diced cucumber, sliced stuffed olives, sliced radishes and chopped walnuts

thick mayonnaise

To garnish

sliced stuffed olives

walnut halves

sliced radishes

lettuce leaves

tomato slices

cooked peas, cooled

Mix the grated cheese with the cucumber, olives, radishes and walnuts. Moisten with enough mayonnaise to make the consistency of very thick whipped cream. Form into a long roll. Garnish with olives, walnuts and radishes and chill well. Arrange the lettuce leaves, tomato slices and peas around the cheese log on a serving dish.

Garlic bread
Serves 4 to 6

Preheat the oven to 350°. Slice a loaf of French bread almost to the base, without cutting right through. Blend ¼ cup (½ stick) butter with garlic salt or crushed garlic and spread it on the bread slices. Wrap the loaf in foil and heat in the oven for 25–30 minutes.

Pineapple soufflé dessert

Serves 4 to 6

¼ cup (½ stick) butter
¼ cup superfine sugar
grated rind and juice of 1 lemon
2 eggs, separated
½ cup self-rising flour, sifted
¾ cup canned pineapple juice

Cream the butter with the sugar and lemon rind. Gradually beat in the egg yolks and flour. Add the lemon and pineapple juices. Fold in the stiffly beaten egg whites. The mixture may look curdled at this stage, but it does not matter.

Preheat the oven to 350°. Pour the mixture into a soufflé dish or baking dish and stand it in a roasting pan containing a little cold water. Bake in the center of the oven for about 40 minutes, or until risen and light brown. Serve hot.

The dessert separates during cooking, giving a sauce layer at the bottom of the dish with a light soufflé mixture on the top.

To vary, serve with rings of hot pineapple or with vanilla ice cream. Use orange juice in place of pineapple juice.

**Speedy bortsch
Sweet and sour ham with
Crispy-topped noodles
Green beans and
tomatoes
Cherry-grapefruit Alaska**
Serves 4

Speedy bortsch
Serves 4

1 medium-sized onion, chopped
1 tablespoon shortening
3¾ cups canned consommé
salt and pepper
1 large cooked beet, grated
yogurt or sour cream, for garnish

Cook the onion in the melted shortening until it is soft but not brown. Add the consommé and heat thoroughly. Season well. Add the beet and heat it through. Spoon the soup into individual bowls and top with a little yogurt or soured cream.

Sweet and sour ham
Serves 4

3 tablespoons butter
2½ tablespoons light brown sugar
3 tablespoons vinegar
3 tablespoons red currant jelly
1–2 teaspoons mustard
good shake of pepper
4 slices cooked ham, ¼–½ inch thick

Place the butter, brown sugar, vinegar and red currant jelly in a skillet and stir over gentle heat until the mixture forms a smooth sauce. Add the mustard and pepper. Add a little salt if the ham is mild in flavor. Add the slices of ham and heat gently. Serve the ham on a bed of crispy-topped noodles and spoon over the sauce.

To vary, add a few drops of Worcestershire sauce or hot-pepper sauce.

Crispy-topped noodles
Serves 4

½ lb ribbon noodles
1 tablespoon butter
½ cup dry bread crumbs
½ cup finely grated sharp Cheddar cheese

Cook the noodles in boiling salted water until tender, then drain them. Toss the noodles in the butter in a heatproof dish and top with the bread crumbs and cheese. Brown for a few minutes under the broiler or in the oven.

Green beans and tomatoes
Serves 4

1 lb green beans, thawed if frozen
3–4 tomatoes, peeled and sliced
salt and pepper

Cook the beans in boiling salted water until tender. Drain the beans and put them in a saucepan with the tomatoes and seasoning. Heat for a few minutes and serve.

To vary, cook a chopped onion in butter for 5 minutes, then add the cooked beans and the tomatoes to the skillet and turn them in the onion and butter. Alternatively, add chopped fresh herbs to the saucepan with the tomatoes.

Cherry-grapefruit Alaska
Serves 4

2 good-sized grapefruit
1 can (about 8 oz) black cherries, drained
3 egg whites
½ cup superfine sugar
vanilla ice cream

Preheat the oven to 450°. Cut the grapefruit in half and remove the segments. Discard the pith, the membrane around the segments and the seeds. Put the grapefruit pieces back in the shell with some of the cherries and sweeten to taste. Beat the egg whites until very stiff and gradually beat in the sugar. Place a scoop of ice cream on each grapefruit half and spoon over the meringue mixture. Decorate with a few cherries. Bake in the oven for 5 minutes.

To vary, use halved and pitted grapes in place of cherries.

Citrus fruit cocktails
Broiled flounder
Cauliflower niçoise
Gingerbread with
apple sauce
Serves 4

Citrus fruit cocktails
Serves 4

juice of 1 large grapefruit
juice of ½ lemon
juice of 4 large oranges
sugar or honey, to taste
few bruised mint leaves, if available

Mix all the fruit juices and sweeten to taste with sugar or honey. Add a few bruised mint leaves, if available. Serve in long-stemmed glasses.

Note: If you wish to frost the glasses, dip the rims in lightly beaten egg white, then in sugar.

Cauliflower niçoise
Serves 4

1 medium-sized cauliflower, in flowerets
salt and pepper
¼ cup (½ stick) butter
2 medium-sized onions, chopped
4 large tomatoes, peeled and chopped
1 teaspoon cornstarch
2 anchovy fillets, chopped

Cook the cauliflower in boiling salted water until tender. Meanwhile, melt the butter in a skillet and cook the onions until soft. Add the tomatoes and cook to a thick purée. Mix the cornstarch with about ¾ cup of the cooking liquid from the cauliflower and add it to the tomato mixture with the anchovy fillets. Cook until thickened and spoon the sauce over the cauliflower.

Note: Green beans or broccoli may also be served in this way.

Broiled flounder
Serves 4

4 medium-sized flounder, soaked in a little milk for 30 minutes
butter
To garnish
parsley sprigs
lemon wedges

Drain the fish and brush with melted butter. Broil on both sides until tender. Garnish with parsley sprigs and lemon wedges.

Gingerbread
Serves 4

2 cups self-rising flour
¾ teaspoons baking soda
1 teaspoon cinnamon
2 teaspoons ground ginger
½ cup (1 stick) butter
⅔ cup dark brown sugar
⅔ cup plus 2 tablespoons dark molasses
2 eggs, beaten
¼ cup milk

Preheat the oven to 325°. Sift the dry ingredients together into a large mixing bowl. Melt the butter in a large saucepan with the sugar and molasses, then add the mixture to the flour. Beat in the eggs and milk. Pour the mixture into a 8-inch square pan lined with greased waxed paper. Bake in the center of the oven for 1¼ hours. Let the cake cool in the pan. Cut into squares for serving.

Serve apple sauce separately.

Apple sauce
Serves 4

Simmer 1-pound sliced apples in a little water with sugar to taste. Strain or purée in a blender.

Desserts

Berry mold
Serves 4 to 6

1 cup strawberries, hulled
2 cups black cherries, pitted
2 cooking apples, pared, cored and sliced
¾–1 cup superfine sugar
6–8 slices white bread, crusts removed
½ cup heavy cream, lightly whipped for serving

Reserve a few strawberries and cherries for decoration. Put the rest of the fruit in a saucepan with the sugar. Cover and heat very gently until the juices run from the fruit. Stir occasionally to prevent the fruit from sticking.

Line a 5-cup bowl or mold with the slices of bread, keeping some bread for the top. Fill the lined bowl with the fruit and cover with bread. Place a saucer or small plate on top, press it down until the juice comes to the surface, then put a weight on it. Chill overnight. Turn out, decorate with reserved fruit and serve with the lightly whipped cream.

Mocha pots
Serves 8

6 eggs, separated
2 tablespoons butter
6 oz (6 squares) semi-sweet chocolate
1½ tablespoons rum
3 tablespoons coffee extract
3 tablespoons heavy cream

Put the egg yolks, butter and chocolate in the top of a double boiler. Cook gently, stirring occasionally, until the chocolate has melted. Remove from the heat and beat in the rum and coffee extract.

Beat the egg whites until stiff and fold them into the chocolate mixture. Pour into eight small ramekin dishes or pots and leave in a cool place to set. Whip the cream until thick and pipe to decorate each pot. Serve with crisp sweet cookies.

Opposite left: Berry mold
Left: Mocha pots

Stuffed figs
Serves 4

4 fresh figs
1 cup ricotta, cottage or cream cheese
1 large egg, separated
¼ cup sugar
1–2 tablespoons kirsch or brandy
almonds, to decorate

Wipe the figs and cut downwards into quarters, just enough to be able to open out the fruit – take care not to cut right through. Put the cheese in a mixing bowl; if using cottage cheese, strain it. Add the egg yolk and sugar to the cheese and beat until the mixture is light and creamy. Then add the kirsch or brandy.

Beat the egg white until it is stiff and fold it into the cheese. Spoon the mixture into the center of the figs and decorate each one with an almond. Chill before serving.

Orange cheesecake
Serves 6 to 8

¼ cup (½ stick) butter
1 tablespoon clear honey
grated rind of 2 oranges
¼ cup superfine sugar
1½ cups graham cracker crumbs
For the filling
¼ cup (½ stick) butter
grated rind of 1 orange
¼ cup superfine sugar
2 eggs, separated
¼ cup cornstarch
1½ cups cottage cheese, strained
2 tablespoons orange juice
For decoration
little sifted confectioners' sugar
1 can (about 8 oz) mandarin orange segments, drained

Make the crust: Cream the butter, honey, orange rind and sugar together. Mix in the crumbs and press into an 8-inch springform pan. Preheat the oven to 325°. Make the filling: Cream the butter, orange rind and sugar together. Mix in the egg yolks, cornstarch, cottage cheese and orange juice. Then fold in the stiffly beaten egg whites. Spoon the mixture into the crumb crust and bake in the center of the oven for about 1¼ hours, or until firm and pale golden. Leave the cake to cool in the oven with the heat turned off (to prevent it sinking). Remove the cake from the pan. Sprinkle with confectioners' sugar and decorate with drained mandarin orange segments.

Apple charlotte
Serves 4

4 large cooking apples
juice of ½ lemon
¼ cup (½ stick) butter
1 cup fresh bread crumbs
½ cup light brown sugar
½ teaspoon cinnamon
grated rind of ½ lemon
1 tablespoon water
For decoration
1 red dessert apple
extra lemon juice and rind

Preheat the oven to 400°. Pare the cooking apples, grate them coarsely and sprinkle with lemon juice. Grease a baking dish with some of the butter. Mix the bread crumbs, sugar, cinnamon and lemon rind and put a third of it in the base of the dish. Cover with half the apples, then sprinkle with a third of the crumb mixture and dot with half the remaining butter. Cover with the rest of the apples and add the water. Sprinkle with the rest of the crumb mixture and dot with the remaining butter. Cover with foil and bake in the oven for about 45 minutes, then remove the foil to brown. Decorate with apple slices dipped in lemon juice and grated lemon rind.

Above: Stuffed figs
Opposite top: Apple charlotte
Opposite bottom: Orange cheesecake

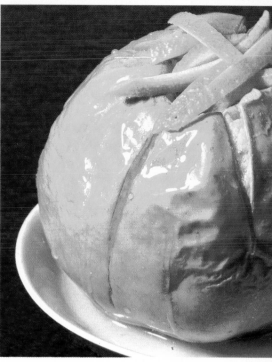

Caramel custard
Serves 4 to 6

$\frac{3}{4}$ cup superfine sugar

3 tablespoons water

For the custard

$2\frac{1}{2}$ cups milk

4 eggs

1 tablespoon sugar

Make the caramel sauce: Put the superfine sugar in a heavy-bottomed saucepan with the water. Stir over very low heat until the sugar dissolves. If the sugar and water splash against the sides of the pan, brush with a pastry brush dipped in cold water – this helps prevent the mixture crystalizing. Allow the sugar and water to boil steadily until golden brown, then use it to coat an 8-inch oval or round ovenproof dish. Turn the dish around to make sure the bottom and sides are evenly coated.

Preheat the oven to 300°. Make the custard: Heat the milk in a saucepan to scalding – do not let it boil. Beat the eggs and sugar together in a bowl, then add the heated milk, stirring constantly. Pour the custard into the caramel-coated dish and stand it in a baking pan containing cold water. Bake in the coolest part of the oven for 1½–2 hours until the custard is firm. Leave it to cool in the dish for about 10 minutes, then invert it onto a serving dish.

Baked apples
with orange filling
Serves 4

4 large cooking apples

2 tablespoons orange jelly or marmalade

finely grated rind of 1 orange

2 tablespoons orange juice

sugar to taste

strips of orange rind, to decorate

Preheat the oven to 350°. Remove the cores from the apples and make a slight slit in the skin round the center to stop the apples bursting. Place the apples in an ovenproof dish and fill the centers with the marmalade, orange rind and juice. Add sugar to taste.

Bake the apples in the center of the oven for about 1 hour. Decorate with strips of orange rind.

Above left: Caramel custard
Above right: Baked apples with orange filling
Opposite left: Banana and lemon cream
Opposite right: Orange water ice

Banana and lemon cream
Serves 6

1 package lemon-flavored powdered gelatin
1¾ cups boiling water
5 teaspoons lemon juice
1 tablespoon superfine sugar
1¼ cups heavy cream
2 egg whites, stiffly beaten
5 small bananas
20–24 lady fingers
few candied cherries, to decorate

Dissolve the gelatin in the water and stir in half the lemon juice and all the sugar. Cool until it is just beginning to set. To set it more quickly, stand the bowl over ice cubes, or use ¾ cup hot water to dissolve the gelatin and make up the quantity with iced water. When the gelatin is firm, beat it until frothy, then add most of the cream, whipped until stiff. Fold in the egg whites and three sliced bananas. Spoon into a 5 cup mold (rinsed in cold water). When set, turn out. Press cream-coated lady fingers around the edge and top with the remaining whipped cream, sliced bananas (dipped in the remaining lemon juice) and the candied cherries.

Orange water ice
Serves 6

thinly pared rind and juice of 3 large oranges
thinly pared rind and juice of 1 small lemon
2 cups water
½ cup sugar
2 teaspoons unflavored powdered gelatin
1 egg white

Put the orange and the lemon rind in a saucepan with the water and sugar and simmer for 8 minutes. Soften the gelatin in 2 tablespoons orange juice and add it to the saucepan, stirring until it is dissolved. Then strain the liquid and add it to the remaining fruit juice. Taste and add a little extra sugar if required, but do not make the mixture too sweet.

When the mixture is cool, pour it into an ice cube tray without dividers and freeze. When it is lightly frosted, remove it and blend it with the stiffly beaten egg white. Freeze again until firm. Serve in glasses or in orange skins, as illustrated.

Above: Fruit meringue trifle; Below: Apricot fool

Fruit meringue trifle
Serves 6 to 8

2 pints raspberries
sugar, to taste
2 cups heavy cream
¾ cup white wine
8 medium-sized meringue shells

Put the raspberries in a bowl and sprinkle with sugar. Whip the cream until it holds its shape. Reserve a little cream for decoration. Gradually blend the wine with the remaining cream and sweeten to taste. Break the meringue shells into fairly large pieces and put a layer at the bottom of a serving bowl. Add half the fruit, then the cream and wine mixture, then most of the remaining fruit – keep a little for decoration. Top with meringue pieces, piped cream and reserved raspberries. Serve within an hour of preparation so that the meringue stays crisp.

Note: The trifle can also be made with sliced fresh peaches, apricots or pears.

Apricot fool
Serves 4

1 cup dried apricots, soaked overnight in 1¼ cups water and the juice of 1 lemon
sugar to taste
¾ cup heavy cream or plain yogurt
toasted slivered almonds, to decorate

Simmer the apricots in the soaking water and lemon juice until they are tender. Strain them or purée in a blender and sweeten with sugar to taste. Blend the apricot purée with the whipped cream or yogurt. Spoon into four glasses and top with almonds.

Steamed apple tower
Serves 6

2 cups self-rising flour
pinch of salt
½ cup chopped suet, butter or margarine
water to mix
1 cup whipped cream, to serve
For the filling
2 tablespoons light corn syrup
1 jar (about 8 oz) mincemeat
3 large cooking apples, pared, cored and grated

Sift the flour and salt together. Mix in the suet, or rub in the butter or margarine and bind with enough water to give a rolling consistency. Roll out the dough very thinly. Cut it into four circles: Make one circle the size of the base of a bowl with 5 cups capacity. Make another circle almost the size of the top of the bowl and two circles of intermediate sizes.

Grease the bowl and put the syrup in the bottom, then put in the smallest circle of dough. Add one-third of the mincemeat mixed with one-third of the apple. Then put in the next size of dough circle topped with mincemeat and apple. Add the third circle of dough topped with mincemeat and apple. Top with the largest round of dough and cover with greased paper, then foil. Steam over boiling water for 2½ hours. Turn out and serve with cream.

129

Pineapple mousse

Serves 4

3 eggs, separated
juice of 1 lemon
$\frac{1}{4}$ cup superfine sugar
$\frac{1}{2}$ tablespoon unflavored powdered gelatin
$1\frac{1}{4}$ cups canned pineapple juice
$\frac{1}{2}$ cup heavy cream
extra cream, to decorate

Put the egg yolks, lemon juice and sugar in the top of a double boiler over simmering water and beat until thick and pale. Remove from the heat and leave to cool, beating occasionally.

Put the gelatin and $\frac{1}{4}$ cup of the pineapple juice in a small heatproof bowl and place over simmering water. Stir to dissolve the gelatin, then add the remaining pineapple juice. Stir into the egg yolk mixture. Leave in a cool place until it is just beginning to set, stirring frequently.

Whip the cream until it is thick, then fold into the pineapple mixture. Beat the egg whites until stiff and fold them into the mixture. Turn the mousse into a serving dish and put in the refrigerator to set. Decorate with rosettes of whipped cream.

Iced mixed fruit dessert

Serves 6

$2\frac{1}{2}$ cups milk
1 cup marshmallows
1 teaspoon cocoa powder
1 teaspoon instant coffee
$\frac{1}{2}$ cup raisins
1 tablespoon currants
2 tablespoons dry sherry
$\frac{1}{2}$ cup chopped Maraschino cherries
$\frac{1}{2}$ cup chopped nuts
$1\frac{1}{4}$ cups heavy cream
confectioners' sugar, sifted
extra Maraschino or candied cherries, to decorate

Put the milk, marshmallows, cocoa and coffee into a saucepan and heat gently until the marshmallows are almost melted. Then allow to cool. Meanwhile, mix the dried fruit with the sherry. Leave the fruit to stand for 30 minutes, then add it to the marshmallow mixture with the cherries and nuts. Freeze for a short time until the mixture is slightly thickened. Then fold in the whipped cream and turn the mixture into a chilled bowl. Freeze until firm.

Turn the pudding out, sprinkle with confectioners' sugar, decorate with cherries and serve with whipped cream and crisp cookies.

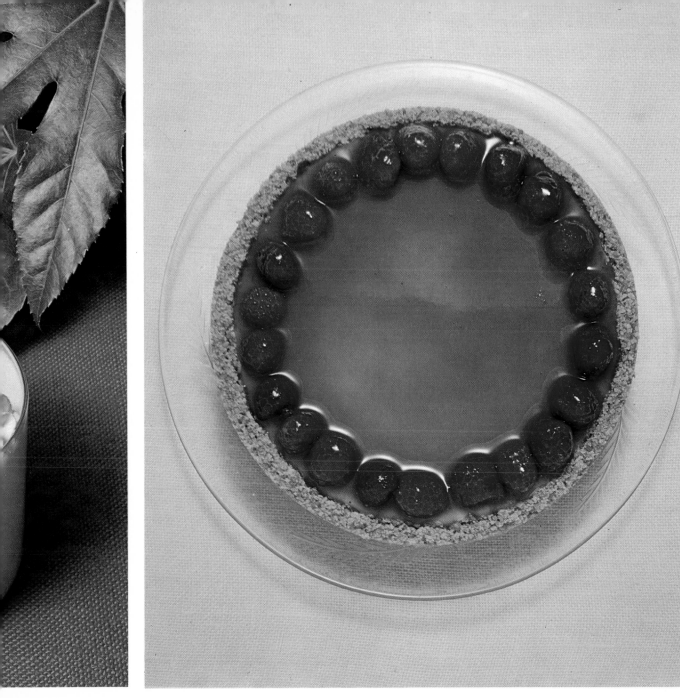

Opposite bottom: Iced mixed fruit dessert; Above left: Pineapple mousse; Above right: Chilled raspberry cheesecake

Chilled raspberry cheesecake
Serves 6

1 package lemon-flavored powdered gelatin
1½ cups crushed graham crackers
2 tablespoons light brown sugar
½ cup butter, melted
¾ cup heavy cream
2 packages (about 8 oz each) cream cheese, softened
juice of 2 lemons
½ cup superfine sugar
For the topping
1 cup raspberries, frozen or fresh
¼ cup red currant jelly

Dissolve the gelatine in 2 tablespoons boiling water. Make up to 1¼ cups with cold water and leave to become cold, thick and nearly set. Mix the crushed graham crackers, brown sugar and melted butter and use the mixture to line the bottom of an 8 or 9-inch springform pan.

Whip the cream until thick. Beat the cream cheese, then gradually beat in the thickened gelatin, lemon juice, cream and superfine sugar. Turn the mixture into the prepared pan and put in the refrigerator to set.

About 30 minutes before serving, arrange the raspberries around the edge of the cheesecake. Melt the red currant jelly over low heat and spoon it over the cheesecake. If necessary, thin the jelly with a little water.

Above: English plum pudding; Centre: Crêpes; Right: Lemon soufflé

English plum pudding

Makes 2 to 3 puddings

English Plum Pudding is a steamed pudding, that the English often eat during the winter. This dessert is very moist because the suet or beef fat melts during cooking. If you are not able to buy suet, use beef fat that has been frozen and then ground in a meat grinder.

1 cup self-rising flour
1 teaspoon ground mixed spice
½ teaspoon cinnamon
½ teaspoon ground nutmeg
1½ cups soft fine bread crumbs
½ cup finely chopped suet, or beef fat
⅔ cup dark brown sugar
2⅔ cups seedless raisins
⅔ cup currants
⅔ cup chopped citron
½ cup chopped blanched almonds
⅔ cup grated cooking apple
grated rind and juice of 1 lemon
2 eggs, beaten
1 cup dark ale, to mix
2 tablespoons brandy or dry sherry

Sift the flour with the spices into a large mixing bowl. Add the bread crumbs, suet or beef fat and sugar. Mix in the fruit, nuts, apple, lemon rind and juice. Then add the eggs with the ale and mix well. Finally, mix in the brandy or sherry.

Divide the mixture between two or three greased small mixing bowls. Cover the top of each bowl with greased foil or paper, making a pleat in the top to allow for expansion. Select a saucepan with a tight-fitting lid, and large enough to hold the bowls. Put a canning rack in the bottom of the saucepan and add enough water to go halfway up the sides of the bowls. Place the bowls on the rack. Bring the water to a boil, cover the saucepan and boil at least 5 hours. Add more water during the cooking time, if necessary. Remove the wet covers and put on dry foil or waxed paper covers and store in a cool, dry place.

Cook the puddings in the same way for 2 to 3 hours before serving. Serve with brandy hard sauce, see recipe below.

Brandy hard sauce

Serves 8 to 10

½ cup (1 stick) sweet butter
1⅓ cups confectioners' sugar, sifted
¼ cup brandy

Cream the butter and sugar together, then mix in the brandy. Chill thoroughly before serving.

Crêpes

Serves 4

1 cup all-purpose flour
pinch of salt
2 eggs, beaten
1¼ cups milk, or milk and water
2 teaspoons melted butter
vegetable oil or shortening, for cooking

Sift the flour and salt into a large mixing bowl. Gradually beat in the eggs and liquid to give a smooth batter. Leave in a cool place for about 30 minutes. Stir in the butter just before cooking.

Put 1–2 teaspoons of vegetable oil or shortening in a skillet or crêpe pan and heat thoroughly. Pour enough batter into the skillet to give a paper-thin layer. Cook quickly for 1–2 minutes until lightly browned on the underside, then turn and cook on the other side. Remove from the skillet, roll up, place on a warm plate and keep warm. Cook all the pancakes in the same way. Serve with sugar and lemon juice, jam or honey.

Note: To make crêpes into Crêpes suzettes, sprinkle with sugar, a little orange juice or Grand Marnier and fold into quarters. Melt a generous quantity of butter in a separate skillet, add Grand Marnier to taste and simmer the crêpes in the sauce for a minute or two on each side. Pour any remaining sauce liquid over the crêpes before serving.

Lemon soufflé

Serves 5 to 6

finely grated rind of 2 lemons
¼ cup lemon juice
3 eggs, separated
½–¾ cup superfine sugar
¾ tablespoon unflavored gelatin
4 tablespoons cold water
1¼ cups heavy cream, stiffly whipped
small ratafia cookies or macaroons to decorate

First prepare a 6-inch soufflé dish: Cut a piece of waxed paper three times the depth of the dish. Fold the paper in half to give a double thickness and tie it around the dish. Brush with melted butter the part that stands above the dish. Put the lemon rind, juice, egg yolks and sugar in the top of a double-boiler and place over very hot water. Beat until thick and creamy. Soften the gelatin in the cold water, add to the lemon-flavored mixture and stir over the heat until the gelatin has dissolved. Cool the mixture until it starts to stiffen, then fold in the cream. Beat the egg whites until stiff, but not too dry, and fold them into the mixture. Spoon it into the prepared soufflé dish.

Leave the soufflé to set, then carefully remove the paper. Crush some of the cookies and press the crumbs around the sides. Decorate the top with the remaining cookies.

Above: Brandy soufflé; Opposite top: Fruit salad; Opposite bottom: Grape meringue tart

Brandy soufflé
Serves 4 to 6

| about 12 lady fingers |
| 6 tablespoons brandy |
| $\frac{3}{4}$ cup chopped candied cherries or mixed candied fruits |
| 2 tablespoons butter |
| $\frac{1}{4}$ cup all-purpose flour |
| $\frac{3}{4}$ cup milk |
| $\frac{1}{2}$ cup light cream |
| $\frac{1}{4}$ cup superfine sugar |
| 3 egg yolks |
| 4 egg whites |

Preheat the oven to 350°. Arrange the lady fingers in the bottom of a soufflé dish and add 3 tablespoons brandy and the cherries or fruit. Melt the butter in a large saucepan. Stir in the flour and cook gently for 2 minutes. Gradually stir in the milk and cream. Bring slowly to a boil, stirring constantly, and cook until thickened. Add the sugar, remaining brandy and the egg yolks. Fold in the stiffly beaten egg whites. Pile the mixture over the lady fingers. Bake for 40 minutes in the center of the oven. Serve at once.

Grape meringue tart
Serves 4 to 6

| $\frac{1}{4}$ cup ($\frac{1}{2}$ stick) butter |
| $\frac{1}{2}$ cup dark brown sugar |
| $\frac{1}{4}$ cup light brown sugar |
| $\frac{1}{2}$ cup light corn syrup |
| 1 cup bran buds |
| small meringues, to decorate |
| **For the filling** |
| $\frac{1}{4}$ cup apricot jam, strained |
| 3 tablespoons water |
| 2 cups white grapes, halved and pitted |
| $\frac{1}{4}$ cup black grapes, halved and pitted |

Melt the butter, the sugars and syrup in a large saucepan and stir to mix. Remove from the heat and stir in the bran buds. Press the mixture into an 8-inch springform pan or pie plate. Leave in a cool place for 2–3 hours to harden.

Heat the jam and water in a saucepan to make a glaze. Arrange the grapes in the tart shell and brush with the warm glaze. When the glaze has cooled, arrange the small meringues around the edge. Serve with cream.

To vary, use crushed cookies or flaked corn cereal instead of bran buds.

Fruit salad

Take a selection of dried fruits, such as dates, raisins, prunes and figs. Chop them and soak them in sherry for several hours until they are plump.

Then prepare a selection of fresh fruits, such as oranges, apricots, grapes, apples, pears, bananas and plums. Slice apples, pears and bananas and sprinkle them with lemon juice to prevent discoloration.

Mix all the fruits together, leaving a few to decorate, as in the picture above. Add a little orange juice and some sugar. The mixture should not be too sweet but should be quite moist. Arrange the fruit in a bowl, cover with foil, and chill in the refrigerator for a few hours. Sprinkle with flaked chocolate.

Baked dishes

Brioches
Serves 12

3 tablespoons water
$\frac{1}{2}$ package ($\frac{1}{2}$ oz) active dried yeast
1 tablespoon plus $\frac{1}{2}$ teaspoon superfine sugar
2 cups all-purpose flour
$\frac{1}{2}$ teaspoon salt
2 eggs, beaten
$\frac{1}{4}$ cup ($\frac{1}{2}$ stick) butter, melted and cooled
For the glaze
1 egg, beaten
1 tablespoon cold water
pinch of sugar

Grease a medium brioche pan or 12 muffin pans.
Heat the water until lukewarm and pour into a small
bowl. Beat in the yeast and $\frac{1}{2}$ teaspoon of the
superfine sugar. Leave in a warm place for about 10
minutes, or until frothy.

Sift the flour and salt into a warm bowl. Mix in the
remaining sugar. Stir in the yeast mixture, eggs and
butter. Beat by hand until the mixture leaves the
sides of the bowl. Knead on a lightly floured board
for 5 minutes. Place the dough in a lightly oiled
plastic bag and leave to rise in a warm place until it
has doubled in size – about 1$\frac{1}{2}$ hours.

Knead the dough well on a lightly floured board for
about 5 minutes. If using muffin pans, divide the
dough into four equal pieces, then each piece into
three. Use about three-quarters of each piece to form
a ball. Place the balls of dough in the pans and firmly
press a hole in the center of each. Place the remaining
small piece of dough in the hole. Place the pans on a
cookie sheet and cover with a large oiled plastic bag.
If using a brioche pan, divide the dough into two
pieces, one about three-quarters of the dough the
other one-quarter. Make up the shape in the same
way as for individual brioches. Leave in a warm place
to rise until light and puffy, about 1 hour.

Preheat the oven to 450°. Mix the ingredients for
the glaze and brush it lightly on the brioches. Bake in
the oven for about 10 minutes. Serve warm.

Right: Brioche
Opposite top: Ring doughnuts and jelly doughnuts

Ring doughnuts and jelly doughnuts
Makes about 12

2 cups all-purpose flour
pinch of salt
2 tablespoons butter
2 tablespoons sugar
1 egg, beaten
$\frac{1}{2}$ cup tepid milk
$\frac{1}{4}$ oz fresh yeast, creamed with 1 teaspoon sugar
jelly (optional)
deep fat, for cooking
superfine sugar

Sift the flour and salt together into a warm bowl. Rub in the butter, add the sugar and make a well in the center. Add the egg and tepid milk to the creamed yeast and put the mixture into the well in the flour. Mix and beat well until smooth. Cover with a cloth and put in a warm place to rise until doubled in bulk, about 30–45 minutes.

Knead the dough well, then turn onto a floured board. To make doughnut rings, roll out the dough and cut out rings. To make balls, roll the dough together into balls.

To fill doughnuts with jelly, make a small depression in the center of each ball, put in a little jelly and close the dough around the jelly. Put the doughnuts on a greased cookie sheet and leave in a warm place until they have doubled in size.

Cook in deep fat until golden brown, then roll in superfine sugar.

Hot cross buns
Makes 12 to 16

$\frac{1}{2}$ oz fresh yeast
$\frac{1}{2}$ cup sugar
generous 1 cup milk or tepid milk and water
4 cups all-purpose flour
pinch of salt
$\frac{1}{2}$ teaspoon ground allspice
$\frac{1}{2}$ teaspoon ground cinnamon
$\frac{1}{4}$ cup ($\frac{1}{2}$ stick) butter
$\frac{1}{2}$ cup dried fruit
For the glaze
$\frac{1}{4}$ cup sugar
2 tablespoons water

Cream the yeast with 1 teaspoon of the sugar. Add the milk, or milk and water, with a sprinkling of flour. Put in a warm place for 15–20 minutes, or until the surface is covered with bubbles.

Meanwhile, sift the flour, salt and spices together in a warm bowl. Rub in the butter, then add the remaining sugar, the dried fruit and lastly the yeast mixture. Knead lightly but well. Cover the dough with a cloth and leave in a warm place to rise. This takes at least 1 hour.

Knead again, then cut the dough into 12–16 pieces and form them into balls. Place them on warmed, lightly greased cookie sheets, mark a cross on each bun with a knife and leave to rise for about 15 minutes.

Preheat the oven to 425°. Bake for about 12 minutes above the center of the oven. Mix the sugar and water for the glaze and brush the buns with it as soon as they come out of the oven.

Note: To make more prominent crosses, pipe on a cross of thick batter before baking.

Danish pastries
Makes 10 to 12

$\frac{3}{4}$ oz fresh yeast
$\frac{1}{4}$ cup sugar
$1\frac{1}{4}$ cups tepid milk, or milk and water
4 cups all-purpose flour
1 cup (2 sticks) butter
1 egg, beaten
For the filling
Jelly, honey, marmalade or thick apple sauce
For the frosting
$1\frac{1}{3}$ cups confectioners' sugar, sifted
little water
candied cherries and/or chopped nuts, to decorate

Cream the yeast with 1 teaspoon of the sugar. Add the tepid liquid and a sprinkling of flour. Leave in a warm place for 15–20 minutes, or until the surface is covered with bubbles.

Sift the rest of the flour into a warm bowl. Rub in $\frac{1}{4}$ cup of the butter, then add the rest of the sugar. Divide the remaining butter into two portions and leave them at room temperature to soften.

Add the yeast liquid to the flour, then stir in the egg. Mix well. Turn the dough onto a floured board and knead until smooth. Then put it back in the mixing bowl, cover with a cloth and leave to rise for about 1 hour, or until double its original size.

Knead the dough again and roll it out to an oblong shape, about $\frac{1}{2}$-inch thick. Spread it with half the softened butter. Fold in three, turn at a right angle, then roll out once more. Then spread with the remaining butter and fold in three. Turn at a right angle, roll again, then fold and turn. The dough is now ready to use and can be made into different shapes.

One of the most popular shapes is the envelope. Roll out the dough until it is about $\frac{1}{4}$-inch thick. Cut into 4-inch squares. Put a little of the chosen filling in the center of each square. Fold so that the opposite ends of the square come to the center, covering the filling.

Viennese orange shortbreads
Makes 7 to 8

1 cup all-purpose flour
1 cup cornstarch
$\frac{3}{4}$ cup (1$\frac{1}{2}$ sticks) butter
$\frac{2}{3}$ cup confectioners' sugar, sifted
finely grated rind of 1 large orange
extra confectioners' sugar, to decorate
For the filling
finely grated rind of 1 large orange
$\frac{1}{2}$ cup butter
1$\frac{1}{4}$ cups confectioners' sugar, sifted

Preheat the oven to 425°. Put the pastries on warmed greased cookie sheets. Leave in a warm place for 20 minutes to rise. Bake about 12 minutes above the center of the oven, then leave to cool.

Mix the confectioners' sugar with enough water to give a thin coating. Spread the frosting over each pastry. Top with cherries and/or chopped nuts.

Note: There are many other traditional shapes for Danish pastries, and they are all just as easy to make as the envelope shape. For instance, to make Danish *pockets* bring all four corners of the square to the center to overlap the filling. For *cockscombs* cut the dough into rectangles, and put the filling on one end; fold over the other part of the dough and seal, then cut three or four deep slashes along one side.

Sift the flour and cornstarch together into a bowl. Cream the butter, confectioners' sugar and orange rind in a large mixing bowl until very soft and light. Gradually beat in the sifted flour and cornstarch. Put the mixture into a pastry bag with a $\frac{1}{2}$-inch rose tip and pipe out 14–16 neat roses on an ungreased cookie sheet.

Preheat the oven to 350°. Bake in the center of the oven for 15–20 minutes. The shortbreads should crisp without becoming too brown. Leave to cool on the cookie sheet.

Make the filling: cream the orange rind, butter and confectioners' sugar together. Sandwich the shortbreads with the filling and sprinkle the tops with a little extra confectioners' sugar.

Opposite: Hot cross buns and Danish pastries
Above: Viennese orange shortbreads

Date crunchies
Makes 14

1 cup whole-wheat flour	
1½ cups oatmeal	
1 cup (2 sticks) butter	
2 cups pitted dates	
2 tablespoons water	
1 tablespoon lemon juice	
1 tablespoon clear honey	
pinch of cinnamon	

Place the flour and oatmeal in a mixing bowl. Rub in the butter. Divide the mixture in half and press half over the bottom of a greased cake pan.

Preheat the oven to 350°. Simmer the dates with the water until soft. Cool and stir in the lemon juice, honey and cinnamon. Spread the date mixture over the oat mixture in the pan and cover with the remaining oat mixture. Spread smooth. Bake in the oven for 25 minutes. Cut into fingers while still warm. Cool in the pan and remove carefully.

Flapjacks
Makes about 18

½ cup (1 stick) butter	
1 tablespoon light brown sugar	
¼ cup light corn syrup	
2 cups oatmeal	
pinch of salt	

Preheat the oven to 350°. Melt the butter with sugar and syrup in a saucepan. Add the oatmeal and salt and mix well. Spread the mixture smoothly in a rectangular baking pan and bake in the oven for 15–20 minutes, or until golden brown and firm to the touch.

Cut into squares or fingers while warm. Cool in the pan and remove carefully.

*Opposite top: Flapjacks
and Date crunchies
Opposite bottom: Popovers
Right: Biscuits*

Biscuits
Makes about 12

2 cups all-purpose flour
½ teaspoon salt
1 teaspoon baking soda
2 teaspoons cream of tartar
3 tablespoons butter or margarine
about ½ cup milk
butter, for serving
favorite flavored jelly, for serving

Sift the flour, salt, soda and cream of tartar into a bowl. Cut the butter or margarine into small pieces and rub it into the flour until the mixture resembles fine bread crumbs. Bind with enough milk to give a soft, but not wet, dough.

Preheat the oven to 425°. Roll out the dough on a floured board to ½-inch thick. Cut with a biscuit cutter into 2-inch circles. Place the biscuits on a greased cookie sheet and bake in the oven for 10 minutes, or until well risen and golden brown. Serve warm with butter and jelly.

To vary, use half white flour and half whole-wheat flour.

Popovers
Makes 8 to 12

1 cup self-rising flour
pinch of salt
2 eggs, beaten
1 cup milk
2 teaspoons vegetable oil or melted butter

Sift the flour and salt into a large bowl. Beat in the eggs, then gradually beat in the milk to make a smooth batter. Mix in the vegetable oil or melted butter just before cooking.

Preheat the oven to 425°. Half fill greased muffin pans with the batter and bake in the oven 20 minutes. Then lower the temperature to 350° for another 15–20 minutes, or until crisp and brown. Serve immediately with butter and jelly or syrup for breakfast, or plain with roast beef.

Mini pancakes

Makes 10 to 12

1 cup self-rising flour
pinch of salt
1 egg, beaten
$\frac{1}{2}$ cup milk

Sift the flour and salt into a large bowl. Beat in the egg, then gradually beat in the milk to make a smooth batter, adding 1–2 tablespoons more milk, if necessary.

Cook the pancakes on a lightly greased griddle, solid hotplate or in a heavy-bottomed skillet. Heat the griddle, hotplate or skillet and drop spoonfuls of the batter on to it. Cook for 1–2 minutes or until the top surface is covered in bubbles. Then turn with a spatula and cook for the same time on the other side. To test if cooked, press gently with the edge of a knife – if no batter oozes out, it is cooked.

Serve warm with butter and jelly or warmed syrup and bacon and sausages.

Rich dark chocolate cake

1$\frac{1}{2}$ cups superfine sugar
6 tablespoons water
$\frac{3}{4}$ cup cocoa powder
$\frac{3}{4}$ cup milk
1 cup (2 sticks) butter
4 eggs, separated
2 cups self-rising flour
2 teaspoons baking powder
$\frac{3}{4}$ cup heavy cream
$\frac{1}{2}$ cup light cream
confectioners' sugar, to decorate

Put $\frac{1}{4}$ cup of the sugar in a saucepan with the water and cocoa and mix to a thick paste. Cook gently until the mixture is thick and shiny. Stir in the milk and leave to cool.

Preheat the oven to 350°. Cream the butter with the remaining sugar until the mixture is pale and fluffy. Beat in the egg yolks with the chocolate mixture. Sift together the flour and baking powder and fold into the mixture. Beat the egg whites until stiff, then fold into the mixture. Divide the mixture between two 8-inch round cake pans which have been lined with waxed paper. Bake in the oven for about 40 minutes or until the cake springs back when lightly pressed with a fingertip. Turn the cakes out, peel off the paper and cool on a wire rack.

Beat the two types of cream together until thick. Split each cake in half horizontally and use the cream to sandwich the layers together. Sprinkle with a little confectioners' sugar.

Left: Mini pancakes
Opposite: Rich dark chocolate cake

English Christmas cake

Serves 10 to 12

2 eggs, beaten
1 cup soft brown sugar
$\frac{1}{4}$ cup corn oil, plus 1 tablespoon
2$\frac{1}{2}$ cups all-purpose flour
1$\frac{1}{2}$ teaspoons baking powder
pinch of salt
3 tablespoons sweet sherry or port
3$\frac{2}{3}$ cups mixed dried fruit
$\frac{2}{3}$ cup diced mixed candied fruit
$\frac{3}{4}$ cup blanched, chopped almonds
3 tablespoons chopped candied cherries
For the almond paste
1$\frac{1}{2}$ cups ground almonds
1 cup confectioners' sugar, sifted
1 egg, beaten
$\frac{1}{4}$ teaspoon almond extract
$\frac{1}{4}$ teaspoon vanilla
little lemon juice
apricot jelly, melted and strained
For the royal frosting
3 egg whites
4 cups confectioners' sugar, sifted
2 teaspoons fresh lemon juice
1 teaspoon glycerine

Grease an 8-inch round cake pan and line the bottom and sides with waxed paper.

Beat together the eggs, brown sugar and oil. Sift the flour with the baking powder and salt and stir it into the egg mixture. Add the sherry or port. Fold in the dried and candied fruit, almonds and cherries. Put the mixture in the prepared pan and level the top with a spatula.

Preheat the oven to 300°. Bake in the center of the oven for 2$\frac{1}{2}$–3 hours, or until a skewer inserted in the center comes out clean. Leave in the pan for at least 15 minutes before turning out onto a wire rack to cool.

When the cake is completely cold, wrap it in foil and leave it for at least a week to mature before covering with the almond paste.

Make the almond paste: Place all the ingredients, except the apricot jelly, in a bowl and mix well to form a stiff paste. Then knead until smooth. Roll out one-third of the paste to a circle large enough to cover the top of the cake. Brush the top of the cake with the apricot jelly and cover with almond paste. Trim the edges. Roll out the remaining almond paste into a long strip the length and width of the sides of the cake. Brush the sides with apricot jelly and cover with almond paste. Seal the seam. Allow the almond paste to dry for 3–4 days before frosting.

Make the frosting: Beat the egg whites until frothy. Add the confectioners' sugar, a little at a time, beating well until the frosting stands up in peaks when the beaters are lifted out of the bowl. Beat in the lemon juice and glycerine. Cover with a damp cloth to prevent the frosting hardening.

Stand the cake on a board, securing it with a little frosting, then cover the top and sides thickly with about three-quarters of the frosting. For a snow effect, press the back of a teaspoon into the icing and lift up so that small peaks form.

If liked, smooth the middle of the cake with a spatula dipped in hot water, then pipe a border of rosettes around the smooth portion. Repeat around the lower edge.

Decorate with ribbon, holly and Christmas ornaments.

Apple crumble cake

4$\frac{1}{2}$ cups self-rising flour
pinch of salt
$\frac{2}{3}$ cup soft light brown sugar
$\frac{1}{2}$ cup chopped pitted dates
3 tablespoons molasses
1$\frac{1}{4}$ cups apple juice or cider
2 eggs, beaten
For the nut topping
3 tablespoons butter
1$\frac{1}{2}$ tablespoons all-purpose flour
3 tablespoons superfine sugar
3 tablespoons chopped walnuts
$\frac{1}{2}$ teaspoon cinnamon
3 tablespoons plum jelly

Grease a 9-inch square cake pan. Line the base and sides with waxed paper.

Preheat the oven to 325°. Sift the flour and salt into a bowl. Add the sugar and dates. Heat the molasses and apple juice or cider gently until the molasses has dissolved. Stir the apple juice or cider mixture and eggs into the flour and mix well. Put the mixture into the prepared pan and bake in the center of the oven for 30 minutes.

Make the topping: Rub together the butter, flour and sugar. Mix in the walnuts and cinnamon.

Remove the cake from the oven, spread it with jelly and sprinkle with the nut topping. Return the cake to the oven for a further 20 minutes, or until a skewer inserted in the center comes out clean. Leave the cake in the pan for 10 minutes, then turn it out onto a wire rack. When completely cold, wrap it in foil and keep for two days before cutting.

Opposite top: English Christmas cake
Opposite bottom: Apple crumble cake

Family fruit loaf

Makes about 10 slices

2 cups self-rising flour
pinch of salt
$\frac{1}{2}$ cup shortening or margarine
just under $\frac{1}{2}$ cup superfine sugar
1 cup diced mixed candied fruit
1 teaspoon finely grated orange rind
1 egg, beaten
about $\frac{1}{2}$ cup cold milk, to mix

Grease a 1 lb loaf pan. Line the bottom and sides of the pan with waxed paper.

Sift the flour and salt into a bowl. Cut in the shortening, then rub it in finely with the fingertips. Add the sugar, fruit and orange rind. Toss the ingredients lightly together. Using a fork, mix to a semi-stiff batter with the egg and milk, stirring briskly without beating. When evenly mixed, put the mixture in the prepared pan.

Preheat the oven to 350°. Bake just above the center of the oven for 1–1$\frac{1}{4}$ hours or until well risen and golden, or until a skewer inserted into the center comes out clean. Leave in the pan for 20 minutes, then turn out onto a wire rack. Peel away the paper. Serve warm or chilled with sweet butter.

Ginger tea loaf

Makes about 12 slices

2$\frac{1}{2}$ cups self-rising flour
2 teaspoons ground ginger
$\frac{1}{2}$ teaspoon ground mixed spice
$\frac{2}{3}$ soft light brown sugar
$\frac{1}{4}$ cup shortening
$\frac{1}{4}$ cup light corn syrup, plus 1 tablespoon
$\frac{1}{4}$ cup molasses, plus 1 tablespoon
1 large egg, beaten
6 tablespoons milk

Grease a 4-cup loaf pan. Line with waxed paper, then brush with melted shortening.

Sift the flour, ginger and spice into a bowl. Add the sugar and toss lightly together. Melt the shortening, syrup and molasses over low heat. Add to the dry ingredients with the egg and milk, stirring briskly. When the mixture is smooth, pour it into the prepared pan.

Preheat the oven to 325°. Bake in the center of the oven for 1$\frac{1}{4}$ to 1$\frac{1}{2}$ hours, or until well risen and firm, or until a skewer inserted in the center comes out clean. Leave in the pan for 5 minutes, then cool on a wire rack.

Opposite: Family fruit loaf
Right: Ginger tea loaf
Below right: French chocolate squares

French chocolate squares
Makes 12 to 16

8 oz (8 squares) semi-sweet chocolate
1 lb sugar cookies, crushed
$\frac{1}{4}$ cup superfine sugar
1 cup chopped walnuts
$\frac{1}{4}$ cup ($\frac{1}{2}$ stick) butter
1 tablespoon rum, brandy or strong coffee
1 can (about 4 oz) sweetened evaporated milk
2 eggs, beaten
For the fudge frosting
2 oz (2 squares) semi-sweet chocolate
2 tablespoons butter
3 tablespoons water
1 cup confectioners' sugar

Oil an 8-inch square cake pan. Line with foil,
allowing it to extend about 1-inch above the top edge
of the pan. Brush with melted butter.

Break up the chocolate, put it in the top of a double
boiler over hot water and leave until melted.

Put the crushed cookies in a bowl. Add the sugar
and walnuts. Melt the butter, then stir in the rum,
brandy or coffee and milk. Stir the mixture into the
melted chocolate with the beaten eggs. Pour the
mixture onto the cookie crumbs and stir thoroughly
to combine. Transfer to the prepared pan and
refrigerate overnight, or until firm and set.

Meanwhile, make the fudge frosting. Melt the
chocolate and butter with the water in the top of a
double boiler over hot water. Remove from the heat.
Stir in the sifted confectioners' sugar and beat until
cool and thick.

Ease out of the pan. Peel away the foil and cover
the top with fudge frosting. When set, cut into
squares. Keep any left-over squares in the
refrigerator.

Lemon meringue pie
Serves 8

| pastry for a single crust 8-inch pie shell |
| **For the filling** |
| grated rind and juice of 2 lemons |
| 2½ tablespoons cornstarch |
| ½–1 cup superfine sugar |
| 1–2 tablespoons butter |
| 2 eggs, separated |

Preheat the oven to 400°. Roll out the dough and line a greased 8-inch springform pan. Line with waxed paper or foil, fill with dry beans and bake in the oven for about 15 minutes, or until the pastry is just set. Cool.

Make the filling: Measure the lemon juice and make up 1¼ cups with cold water. Mix the cornstarch with the lemon juice and water and put in a saucepan with the grated rind and ¼–½ cup sugar, according to taste. Add the butter and stir over gentle heat until the mixture has thickened. Remove from the heat and add the beaten egg yolks. Cook gently for several minutes. Taste and add more sugar, if wished. Spoon the mixture into the pastry shell.

Beat the egg whites until very stiff, then gradually beat in ¼ cup of the remaining sugar. Fold the rest in tablespoon by tablespoon. For a softer meringue, gradually fold in all the sugar. If you want a firm meringue, use an electric mixer and gradually beat in all the sugar. Spoon the meringue over the lemon mixture so that it touches the pastry rim.

To serve freshly cooked: Preheat the oven to 350°. Use the smaller quantity of sugar and brown for 20 minutes in the oven, or cook for 5–8 minutes in a oven preheated to 425°.

To serve cold: Preheat the oven to 250°. Use the larger quantity of sugar and bake for at least 1 hour in the center of the oven.

Above: Lemon meringue pie
Opposite: Vanilla slices

Vanilla slices
Makes 5 to 6 slices

| 2 sheets (17¼ oz package) frozen puff pastry, thawed |
| **For the filling** |
| 1¼ cups heavy cream |
| sugar, to taste |
| few drops of vanilla |
| cherry jelly |
| little sifted confectioners' sugar |

Roll out the pastry on a floured board until paper thin. Cut into 15–18 fingers. Put the fingers of dough on greased cookie sheets and leave in a cool place for about 30 minutes. Preheat the oven to 475°. Bake just above the center of the oven for about 10 minutes, or until risen and golden. Then lower the heat to 325°, or switch off, and cook for a further 5 minutes.

Allow the pastry to cool, then trim the edges with a sharp knife. Whip the cream until thick and add sugar to taste and a little vanilla. Spread one-third of the slices with the cream. Top with another slice, then the jelly and then a final pastry slice. Dust with confectioners' sugar.

Cream horns
Makes 12

2 sheets (17½ oz package) frozen puff pastry, thawed
beaten egg, for glaze
sugar, for dredging
For the filling
strawberry jam
1¼ cups heavy cream
1 teaspoon vanilla
1 tablespoon confectioners' sugar, sifted
2 tablespoons milk
strawberries, hulled, to decorate

Grease 12 cream horn molds. Rinse a large cookie sheet with water and leave it damp.

Roll out the pastry thinly and cut into 12 long strips, about 1 in wide. Brush one side of each strip with water. Wind each strip, with dampened side inside, around the molds, starting from the pointed end and overlapping the strip slightly so that there are no gaps. Place on the cookie sheet, brush with beaten egg and sprinkle with sugar. Leave in a cool place for 30 minutes.

Preheat the oven to 450°. Bake the horns just above the center of the oven for 20–25 minutes, or until golden brown and puffy. Gently lift each horn onto a wire rack to cool.

When the pastry is almost cold, carefully remove the molds. Put a little jam into the pointed end of each pastry horn. Whip the cream with the vanilla, confectioners' sugar and milk until thick. Fill the horns. Decorate each one with a strawberry.

Fruit tarts
Makes 20 to 24

pastry for a single crust 9-inch pie shell
For the filling
selection of fruit such as pears, apples, grapes
lemon juice
¾ cup apricot jelly
candied cherries

Preheat the oven to 400°. Roll out the dough on a lightly floured board and use to line 20–24 tart pans. Place small circle of waxed paper in each tart shell and fill each with dry beans. Bake the shells in the oven for about 20 minutes, or until cooked and golden. Cool on a wire rack.

Meanwhile, prepare the fruit: Pare, core and slice the pears thinly and dip each slice in lemon juice. Do the same with apples, but leave the peel on if it is red. Halve and pit the grapes.

Heat the apricot jelly in a small saucepan with a few drops of lemon juice. Stir until blended, then strain. Fill the cooked tart shells with the prepared fruit and brush with the apricot glaze. Decorate with cherries.

Above: Fruit tarts
Opposite: Cream horns

Apple strudel
Serves 4 to 6

1½ cups all-purpose flour
pinch of salt
1 tablespoon vegetable oil
1 egg, beaten
¼ cup warm water
melted butter, to glaze
confectioners' sugar, for dredging
For the filling
vegetable oil
⅔ cup fresh bread crumbs
⅓ cup golden raisins
4 large cooking apples, pared, cored and chopped
¼ cup sugar, or to taste
grated rind and juice of ½ lemon
1 teaspoon cinnamon

Sift the flour and salt together into a bowl. Add the vegetable oil, egg and water to make a soft dough. Knead well until smooth. Leave covered for 30 minutes. Roll out half the dough at a time on a floured sheet of paper. Roll until paper thin. Brush with oil and sprinkle with bread crumbs.

Preheat the oven to 425°. Mix the rest of the filling ingredients and spread half of the mixture on the dough to within ½-inch of the edge. Wet the edges and roll up, using the waxed paper to help. Seal the edges and place on a greased cookie sheet. Brush with melted butter. Repeat the process with the rest of the dough and filling.

Bake in the oven 40 minutes. Turn the oven down after 30 minutes if the pastry is getting too brown. Cut into pieces and sprinkle with sifted confectioners' sugar.

Above: Apple strudel
Below: Traditional English Christmas pies
Opposite: Profiteroles

Traditional English Christmas pies
Makes 12

pastry for a double crust 9-inch pie shell
1 jar (about 1 lb) mincemeat
beaten egg, for glazing
confectioners' sugar, for dusting

Lightly grease 12 muffin pans. Preheat the oven to 400°. Roll out the pastry on a floured board and cut out 12 circles to fit the muffin pans. Line the muffin pans and fill with mincemeat. Moisten the edges of the pastry with water. Cut out 12 smaller circles for lids and place them on top of the pies. If wished, cut out a star in the center of the lid. Pinch the edges of the pastry together to seal. Brush the tops with beaten egg.

Bake just above the center of the oven for 20 minutes. Remove from the pans when just warm and sprinkle a little sifted confectioners' sugar over the top.

Profiteroles

Makes 20

One of the most elegant of all the delicate French desserts, profiteroles are made from choux pastry. This is a light, rich pastry that is also used for chocolate eclairs.

Cream-filled profiteroles are guaranteed to impress and surprisingly easy to make. The key to making successful choux pastry is to stop beating as soon as the smooth, shiny paste is formed. If the mixture is overbeaten the fat will separate out.

It is best to make the profiteroles on the day of serving, and leave the filling until the last possible moment.

$\frac{1}{4}$ cup ($\frac{1}{2}$ stick) butter

$\frac{1}{2}$ cup milk and water, plus extra if needed

good $\frac{1}{2}$ cup all-purpose flour, sifted

2 eggs, beaten

For the filling and frosting

$1\frac{1}{4}$ cups heavy cream, lightly whipped

$1\frac{1}{3}$ cups confectioners' sugar

1 tablespoon cocoa powder

1 tablespoon rum

1–2 tablespoons warm water

Preheat the oven to 425°. Put the butter, milk and water in a small saucepan and bring to a boil. Remove the saucepan from the heat. Add the flour, all at once, and beat the mixture until it forms a ball. Gradually beat in the eggs to make a smooth, shiny paste. Put the mixture in a large pastry bag fitted with a $\frac{1}{2}$-inch plain tip. Pipe 20 balls onto a greased cookie sheet. Bake in the oven for 10 minutes, then reduce the temperature to 375° and cook for a further 15–20 minutes, or until golden brown.

Make a split with a sharp knife on one side of each profiterole to allow the steam to escape. Cool on a wire rack.

Fill each profiterole with whipped cream. Sift the confectioners' sugar with the cocoa into a bowl. Stir in the rum and sufficient warm water to make a thick glacé frosting. Spear each with a fork and dip the tops in the frosting. Pile up in a pyramid as each one is finished or, if you wish to serve the profiteroles individually, frost the tops and keep separate.

Drinks

Grenadine grape
Serves 2

1¼ cups grape juice
1 tablespoon grenadine
1 egg white
crushed ice
soda water

Thoroughly shake the grape juice, grenadine and egg white with crushed ice. Strain into two glasses and fill with soda.

Above: Grenadine grape
Centre: Apple flame
Right: Whisky cola (left)
and Apricot cooler (right)

Apple flame
Serves 6

1 cup Calvados or apple juice
2 tablespoons Angostura bitters
5 cups boiling water
12 whole cloves
pared rind and juice of 2 lemons
¼ cup Calvados, to flame

Put the Calvados or apple juice, bitters, boiling water, cloves, lemon rind and juice in a saucepan over low heat. Heat well. The mixture should not boil. Carefully pour extra Calvados over the back of a spoon so that it floats on the surface. Set alight and serve immediately.

Whisky cola

Serves 1

$\frac{1}{4}$ cup Scotch whisky
1 tablespoon Curaçao
1 tablespoon lemon juice
2 dashes of Angostura bitters
crushed ice
cola
twist of orange rind, to garnish

Mix the whisky, Curaçao, lemon juice and Angostura bitters in a glass. Add a heaped spoon of crushed ice and fill with cola. Garnish with orange rind.

Apricot cooler

Serves 1

crushed ice
1 stewed or canned apricot
2$\frac{1}{2}$ tablespoons apricot-flavored brandy
1 tablespoon lemon juice
1 teaspoon confectioners' sugar

Pack a tumbler two-thirds full with crushed ice. Strain the apricot and mash well with a fork. Shake the apricot pulp with the apricot brandy, lemon juice and sugar. Add ice to shaker, shake again and pour, unstrained, into the glass.

Above: Glühwein; Above right: Peach froth; Opposite left: Apple power; Opposite right: Chocolate-mint shake

Glühwein
Serves 20

3 bottles dry red wine
½ bottle brandy
1¼ cups water
1¼ cups orange juice
juice of 2 lemons
thinly pared rind of 1 lemon and 1 orange
6 cinnamon sticks
1 orange stuck with 24 cloves

Put all the ingredients in a large saucepan and simmer over low heat. Serve in warm mugs.

Peach froth
Serves 4

2 ripe peaches, peeled, pitted and mashed
½ cup sugar
1½ cups water
1½ cups milk
2 teaspoons clear honey
2 egg whites
ground nutmeg, to garnish

Simmer the peaches with the sugar and water for 45 minutes, then cool and strain. Put in a blender with the milk, honey and egg whites. Blend until frothy. Alternatively, beat vigorously. Chill and serve sprinkled with nutmeg.

Apple power
Serves 4

½ cup apple juice or Calvados
1¼ cups sweet apple cider
¼ cup Grand Marnier
¼ teaspoon ground cloves
¼ teaspoon cinnamon
2 cups crushed ice

Mix all the ingredients in a blender and pour, unstrained, into tall glasses.

If you do not have a blender, shake very thoroughly, allow to stand for several minutes, then shake again before pouring, unstrained, into glasses.

Chocolate-mint shake
Serves 6

5 cups milk
1¼ cups ice cream
½ cup chocolate syrup
¼ cup peppermint syrup
grated chocolate, to decorate

Put all the ingredients, except the grated chocolate, in a blender or shake thoroughly. Pour into glasses and decorate with chocolate.

Index

Acknowledgments

The Publishers would like to thank the following people for their assistance in providing photographs and accessories for this book: American Rice Council: 42, 43; Bryce Attwell: 17, 28, 44, 96; John Searle Austin: 27; Barnaby Picture Library: 44, 45; Birds Eye: 19, 90; Barry Bullough: 14, 15; California Prune Advisory Bureau: 70; Canned and Packaged Foods Bureau: 135; Carrier Cookshops: 115, 116; Chiltonian Ltd.: 7; Cordon Bleu: 92; Crocks Reject China: 70, 71, 114, 115; Dutch Dairy Bureau: 37; Eden Vale Ltd.: 47; Egg Board: 38; Food from France (Sopexa): 94, 103; Fratelli Febbri Editore: 9, 50, 53; Fruit Producers' Council: 24, 79, 93, 125, 151; Melvin Grey: 31, 50, 122, 123, 130, 131, 143; Harvey Nichols: 19; Herring Industry Board: 58; Kellog Co. of Great Britain Ltd.: 135; Paul Kemp: 87, 88; Mike Leale: 52, 68, 72, 101, 110, 117, 119, 129, 130, 134; John Lee: 8, 10, 11, 13, 18, 23, 24, 28, 30, 34, 35, 36, 38, 39, 40, 41, 42, 53, 59, 61, 73, 75, 77, 78, 82, 83, 85, 86, 95, 97, 98, 99, 100, 101, 102, 107, 109, 125, 126, 127, 132, 133, 138, 139, 148, 149; Neil Lorimer: 76, 77; Mazola: 145, 152; David Mellor Ironmonger: 33, 74, 75, 128; National Dairy Council: 127; New Zealand Lamb Information Bureau: 80; Norman Nicholls: 10, 11, 12, 13, 26, 62, 71, 81, 89, 106, 108, 109, 122, 140, 154, 155, 156, 157; PAF International: 9, 17, 29, 32, 46, 47, 48, 56, 57, 61, 79, 94, 98, 124, 136, 137, 146, 147; Pasta Foods Ltd.: 24, 27; Pentangle Photography: 27; Roger Phillips: 2–3; Photopad: 8, 49, 51, 54, 91; Potato Marketing Board: 29; RHM Foods Ltd.: 48, 93, 132, 140, 142; Rice Council: 89, 98; Syndication International: 12, 18, 23, 46, 55, 64, 65, 69, 74, 104, 112, 113, 126, 137, 150: Tabasco Sauce: 99; Taunton Cider: 145; Tupperware: 6, 27; Wedgwood from Gered: 16, 128; John West Foods Ltd.: 20, 58; White Fish Authority: 56; Wilson & Gill: 60, 63.